Teen
Genreflecting

Teen
Genreflecting

Diana Tixier Herald

1997
Libraries Unlimited, Inc.
Englewood, Colorado

To
Chani Ray Herald,
my most beloved teen reluctant reader
and to
Nathan Sundance Herald,
my most beloved avid reader.

Libraries Unlimited, Inc.
P.O. Box 6633
Englewood, CO 80155-6633
1-800-237-6124

Production Editor: Kevin W. Perizzolo
Copy Editor: Kimberly Tanner
Proofreader: Ryan Goldberg
Typesetter: Kay Minnis

Library of Congress Cataloging-in-Publication Data

Herald, Diana Tixier.
    Teen genreflecting / Diana Tixier Herald.
    xii, 134 p. 17x25 cm.
    Includes bibliographical references and index.
    ISBN 1-56308-287-X
    1. Young adult literature, American--Bibliography. 2. Young adult
literature--Stories, plots, etc. 3. Popular literature--Stories,
plots, etc. 4. Fiction genres--Bibliography. 5. Teenagers--Books
and reading. 6. Fiction--Bibliography. 7. Reading interests.
I. Title.
Z1232.H47   1997
[PS490]
016.8130099883--dc20
                                                              96-29139
                                                                    CIP

Contents

Acknowledgments

YALSA, the Young Adult Library Services Association of the American Library Association, deserves high praise for nurturing and training librarians to work with teens. They are also to be thanked for sharing the knowledge of their dedicated members by granting permission to reprint their Genre Lists in this book.

The many members of the Mesa County Public Library District Teen Advisory Board provided invaluable input for the writing of the book. My heartfelt thanks goes to them, especially Nathan, Preston, Rianna, Heather, Della, Amber, Sean, Joshua, Joseph, Nancy, Audra, Liz, Marcus, Cara, Chris, Andrea, and Katie. Liz Campbell, Holly Koelling, and Brian Kenny, the librarians who work with them, also deserve recognition.

 # Introduction

PURPOSE AND USE

This book is a guide for those who help teen readers to identify authors and titles of genre books in libraries and bookstores. It is not intended to identify "safe" or "clean" books for inclusion in censored collections. It is to help find books of interest for teens who read and enjoy genre fiction.

New subgenres, new authors, and new titles appear daily. This guide is only a starting point and should be frequently updated by the user. Scanning book reviews, talking to teens, and reading new genre titles will help keep you current.

SELECTION OF TITLES

This book is not intended to provide comprehensive lists of titles by specific authors. Titles are included to help define a genre. Books by a specific author may fall into various genres or subgenres. Christopher Pike's *Die Softly* is suspense, while his *Remember Me* is definitely in the supernatural realm. Not all works by an author will fall into the same genres.

The titles included all have demonstrated a proven appeal to teen readers. Many titles written for adults but popular with teens have been included. Several of these adult titles have either been included on an annual Best Books for Young Adults list or considered for the list.

Publication Dates

Publication dates are not given. Much genre fiction is timeless but teens are far more conscious of the age of a title than adults. They seem to judge the age of books by the cover art.

Genre fiction with high author recognition allows some books to remain popular long after their cohorts have been forgotten. Lois Duncan's suspenseful books written in the late seventies remain popular, but except for her most dedicated fans, only the titles that have been recently reissued with new cover art go out frequently. Fortunately, some publishers are cognizant of the extreme importance of a contemporary cover to sell a book and are reissuing teen favorites with eye-catching new covers.

SELECTION OF AUTHORS

This guide is not intended to be an all-inclusive compendium of authors writing genre fiction for teens. It is definitely not a scholarly, historical treatise on the subject of genre fiction for teens. Because teen fiction is so volatile it is merely a guide to assist librarians and booksellers to come up with ideas for filling the reading requests of young adults. It is a jumping-off point for finding something to read next.

The authors selected represent those who are popular with teens in the 1990s or authors whose books fit into genre types that are likely to be requested by teens. Most are established but some new authors are included that are expected to grow in popularity. Of course, exciting new genre authors are always exploding onto the scene. Who, in 1985, had ever heard of Christopher Pike or David Eddings, two of the most popular writers now enjoyed by teens?

Teens, Books, Libraries, Publishing, and Booksellers

Contrary to popular belief, teens do read. They do use libraries and they do peruse the racks in bookstores. Unfortunately, this group is frequently overlooked as consumers or even actively ignored. Few libraries and bookstores try to attract a young clientele, while some others actively try to dissuade the teen trade.

It is not uncommon to see signs in the windows of stores near middle schools and high schools limiting the number of students allowed in at any one time. Even some bookstores in close proximity to schools have chosen to go this route.

While visiting with a librarian who manages a multibranch public library system in a major city, I was dismayed to find that this particular system believed that all teen reading needs should be met by school libraries. They felt that public libraries are not in the business of "supplementing" curriculum and therefore they did not select young adult (YA) materials or present YA programs.

Teens are multifaceted individuals with many and varied reading needs. Many read for pleasure or escapism or even to learn what is not taught in school. The idea that tax funding of school districts is sufficient for youth libraries is flawed. For example, should public libraries not select business materials because good companies have their own special libraries?

If we value reading as an intrinsically good activity, we should want to pass this on to our youth. Good reading skills are developed by avid reading and avid readers are usually devoted to some segment of the written word that does not get much respect, such as genre fiction. Mary Leonhardt in her book *Parents Who Love Reading, Kids Who Don't* (Crown, 1993), presents a mini quiz asking how "children become fast, fluent, sophisticated readers" and identifies them as being readers whose reading "often, or even always, consists of subliterature—like comic books, horror novels, science fiction, or romances. They may or may not do their schoolwork. But they read constantly." The key to getting teens to read is to provide them with reading material of interest. Reluctant readers will often become avid readers if they find something to read that catches their interests. Patrick Jones, the author

1

of *Connecting Young Adults and Libraries* (Neal-Schuman, 1992), is always quick to recommend that libraries stock plenty of magazines for their teen clientele. Essential magazine titles he lists include *Sassy, Bop, Thrasher*, and *Weekly World News*. Yes, they may look trashy or ephemeral but they are read and loved by legions of teens and therefore are of value. Leonhardt is "convinced that any kind of reading, as long as students find it enthralling, will quickly and significantly raise reading levels."

Teens do have unique needs, different from readers of other ages. They are experiencing a time of self-discovery and reading allows them to try on different roles and personae to help discover who they are. Teen years are tumultuous and escapist reading is an ideal outlet for youthful angst.

Genre fiction fits many of the needs of young adult readers. Selecting a genre to read is a way of dividing up the world of literature into manageable chunks. Teens like to know what they are getting. Just like Oakely sunglasses, Stussy, or JNCO jeans, teens pay attention to the labels on the books they read. In my personal experience teen readers are the only ones who ask for books, not by author or title, but by imprint. Teens have actually asked for books from Harcourt Brace's Gulliver Books line and Henry Holt's Edge imprint. The teens who requested books by imprint had to explain to me that they sometimes found books that were similar in that they were multicultural or historical novels but were by different authors, had different titles, and were not part of a series. As a librarian I expected people to ask for books by author, title, or subject. These teens had found a way of identifying the books they liked in a different fashion. They noticed that the books they liked had the same imprint, books that a specific publisher had considered, all fit into a particular line.

Teens want an identifiable product from which they will get a certain something that they expect. They identify themselves by what they read and can be very definite about it. "I only read romances." "I never read science fiction." "I only read fantasy."

Offering genre collections, identified as such, to teens is one way to make the books they want accessible. By grouping similar books together whether physically, through spine labeling, or by using lists, books of similar appeal can be identified as being in the same group. Teens can browse a genre they know and enjoy, and may find new authors in that area in addition to authors they already like. By grouping genre fiction teens can find new authors that will provide them with many hours of reading enjoyment.

Some of the genres read by teens are different than genres read by adults. Murder mysteries are one of the most popular adult genres; suspense with a supernatural twist is wildly popular with teens. Westerns, on the whole, are not as popular with teens as historical fiction.

Many teen readers, unremarkably enough started off as child readers. Perhaps it was the Hardy Boys or Nancy Drew, still popular after several generations of young readers, that started a love of reading. Some teen readers got hooked on Jessica and Elizabeth Wakefield of Sweet Valley High or on the girls of the Baby Sitters Club series.

Many individuals enter their teens as readers and library users but quit sometime before leaving their teens. Whatever it was that got them reading in the first place is sometimes just not strong enough to keep them reading through their teens. Teen years are busy years, with major distractions and new experiences. Librarians and booksellers really do need to make an effort if they want to see teen readers grow into adult readers. By providing the books they like to read in friendly surroundings, librarians and booksellers can make friends for life.

School librarians frequently question the age appropriateness of books. With genre fiction teens read what they like whether or not it is "age appropriate." This book does not address the suitability of a title or author for certain age or grade levels. It merely provides an avenue for finding similar books that may be enjoyable to the reader of a particular genre.

NATURE OF
TEEN GENRE FICTION

The American Heritage Dictionary of the English Language defines genre as "a category of artistic composition as in music or literature, marked by a distinctive style, form, or content." (Houghton Mifflin, 1992)

Defining novels by genre is a way of grouping titles that are similar in content. Genres for teen fiction are not as narrowly circumscribed as those for adults. Content, such as a specific life situation, as opposed to form or style, is more important in teen genres than form or a prescribed formula. Almost all teen fiction is plot driven.

Teen genre fiction does have many similarities to adult genre fiction and in some genres; fantasy, science fiction, and horror, in particular; teens and adults read many of the same authors and titles. Stephen King is as beloved to some middle schoolers as he is to the legions of his adult fans.

Many authors of teen genre fiction are prolific. R. L. Stine is reputed to churn out a book every twenty-seven days. An equally prolific author of books aimed at adults would probably be forced to rely on pseudonyms or would be thought to be writing too fast. Stephen King wrote for a while under the name Richard Bachman to allow him to publish more than one book in a year while maintaining his reputation and sales.

Author recognition really does sell books to teens. The phenomenally successful Sweet Valley High series is written by several different authors, including best-selling adult author Eileen Goudge, all using the name Kate William. Additional name recognition is generated by including, for example, "created by Francine Pascal" on the cover. This trend is continuing with other "created" series including 18 Pine Street, created by Walter Dean Myers.

Many book series written for teens are not actually series but are more like imprints. R. L. Stine's Fear Street usually features different characters. His series for preteens and younger teens is Goosebumps.

Silk Makowski in her February 1994 VOYA article, "Serious about Series: Selection Criteria for a Neglected Genre" considers series to be a genre unto themselves. She writes,

> Think of it this way. Monographs give you *everything* in one grand experience. Monographs are a one-night stand. Series, on the other hand, are *built for the long haul*. Everything about them, plot, characters, setting, style of writing, even the physical *look* of the book, contributes to that aim, which is to provide you, the reader, with that same grand experience night after night, week after week, year after year, ad infinitum.

COVER ART AND FORMAT

Teens love paperbacks. They look cool and if one does not want to be seen with a book, they are easily hidden. The appearance of a book is far more important to teens than to any other group. They are very conscious of the age appearance of people depicted on the cover. If the people in the cover illustrations appear too young or are wearing outdated apparel, forget it! Sometimes it seems that the cover is the most important part. Fortunately, the publishers of paperbacks usually pay attention to the covers and often a book that didn't hook teens with its hardcover dust jacket hooks them with an appealing paperback cover.

In libraries, paperbacks look pretty ratty after a few circulations. Covering them with clear vinyl or purchasing prebound copies can improve the durability and preserve the appearance. Not cataloging the paperback collections can be a big mistake in dealing with teen paperbacks. Since paperbacks are the preferred format by most teens, it only makes sense to provide accessibility. Many times teens will want to read everything by an author or read a series in order. The ability to find the title in the catalog and place a hold on a book for the patron is important. Also, if a book frequently requested by teens is not in the catalog it is an indication that perhaps it should be purchased.

REVIEWS OF
TEEN GENRE FICTION

Reviews of teen genre fiction can be difficult to find. The major young adult review sources, with the exception of VOYA, do not separate out reviews of genre fiction. Often, the genre is not even mentioned in a review. VOYA, the most comprehensive review source of young adult materials, groups science fiction, fantasy, and horror together, separate from the other fiction reviews. It also publishes an annual list of their reviewer's choices for the best science fiction, fantasy, and horror books. VOYA also does an excellent job of including paperback reviews. Many of the books teens want to read are paperback originals that are sometimes not reviewed anywhere else.

Other review resources include *Booklist, Library Journal, School Library Journal, Bulletin of the Center for Children's Books, Hornbook, Kirkus Children's*

Reviews, and some issues of *Publishers Weekly*. However, plowing through pages and pages of reviews of children's books is often necessary to glean the few reviews of teen books included. Other review sources used by libraries are *Kliatt Young Adult Paperback Book Guide* and *ALAN Review*. (Assembly on Literature for Adolescents of the National Council of Teachers of English.)

PAPERBACK RESOURCES

Publications from large book distributors are by far the most timely resources in discovering what paperback genre titles are being published for teens. *Hot Picks* is the title of the prepublication catalog from Baker and Taylor and *Paperback Advance* the title from Ingram. Another source of information on teen genre authors are the prebound distributors. Catalogs from Permabound and Econoclad hold a wealth of information. Books teens have been asking for that are unfamiliar to the librarian or bookseller can often be found in these excellent catalogs. Publisher's catalogs are also helpful, especially when looking for forthcoming books by the most popular authors or in the most popular paperback series.

In previous years, committees of YALSA, the Young Adult Library Services Association of the American Library Association (ALA), compiled a number of lists of the best genre fiction available in paperback. They had lists available for fantasy, science fiction, horror, romance, sports, humor, and historical works. Those committees no longer exist but the most recent lists are included in the appropriate chapter, courtesy of the Association. A new committee, recently formed within YALSA, will be compiling lists of popular reading for teens. This should be a good resource to watch for.

PROGRAMS FOR TEENS

Teen summer reading games or teen participation councils are excellent ways of meeting teens who read. One of the best ways to know what is going on in teen genre fiction is to talk to teens and find out what they are reading. The really hot authors will come up again and again. Teens were talking about Margaret Weis and Tracy Hickman a year before I ever saw a review for any of their books. The teens had seen the paperback books in game stores and bookstores and, attracted by their covers, had purchased, read, and become fans.

By having some kind of program where you can interact with teens, you will learn a lot and be able to provide them with a larger range of what they want to read.

Teen Advisory Boards

Different teens and different libraries have different ways of working together. Teen Advisory Boards are a way for libraries to obtain feedback from teens on programs and resources. Some Boards plan programs from start to finish, others identify areas in which they would like to see programming, and yet others advise librarians on aspects of programs conceived and implemented by the library staff. A Teen Advisory Board can also work as a book discussion group, providing an up close and personal look at what teens think about what they read.

Often Boards provide willing and able teen volunteers to perform various tasks in the library or related to library programs.

Further information on how to start and run Teen Advisory Boards and similar programs can be found in *Youth Participation in School and Public Libraries: It Works* edited by Carolyn Caywood. (Young Adult Library Services Association, American Library Association, 1995)

Teen Summer Reading Games

Summer reading games are a great way to keep teens coming into the library and bookstore when school is out for the summer. Libraries in different parts of the country have provided teen summer reading games for their young adult patrons. The secret to having a good game is to structure it specifically for teens, making it very different from summer reading games for children.

A Teen Advisory Board is an excellent place to start planning a game. Find out what the teens who use your library would like in a game. When teens at Mesa County Public Library District were polled on what elements would contribute to a teen summer reading game that teens would actually want to play, some of the answers were:

Don't put our names up on the wall.

Have lots of prizes.

Don't breathe down our necks.

No stupid charts!

No stupid forms!

It shouldn't be competitive.

It can be done with friends.

The game that was produced that first summer was simple. Every book that was read by a teen was good for an entry in a weekly prize drawing. Everyone who read six books won a ticket to a skating party. If teens wanted to team up, the team had to read an average of six books each for all team members to win party tickets. A skating rink and radio station cosponsored the game. The weekly prize drawings were held over the air and the radio station and the skating rink both contributed to cover costs of printing the game materials. The only expenses incurred by the library were for staff time. One hundred sixty-eight teens read 1,800 books in eight weeks of the game that first summer.

Enoch Pratt Library and Boulder Public Library have produced elaborate summer reading games. *Bookjack*, a complex game created by Cathi

MacRae, has many different options and ways to play. It was the official Colorado State Young Adult Reading Game in 1990. Copies of the *Bookjack* manual are available for sale. It is a how-to-do-a-young-adult-summer-reading-game book. It has everything one needs to plan and produce a great teen summer reading game.

The Colorado statewide teen summer reading game in 1994 was *Bookquest*. It emphasized genre reading by providing incentives for teens to broaden their horizons by reading in many different genres. The manual included genre lists to assist readers in finding titles. The game was conceived by a Teen Advisory Board, and refined and implemented by librarian members of YALA, Young Adult Librarians Anonymous. Teens created the basic design for the graphics.

Author Visits

Readers love to see and hear their favorite authors. Author visits can sometimes be arranged in cooperation with secondary schools. The visits escalate the popularity of the author's books and frequently other books in the same genre.

Teen Volunteers

Mesa County Public Library District has a very successful volunteer program, in fact, volunteers shelve all materials at its main library. Teen volunteers shelving the teen materials often booktalk to teens using the collection. Teen volunteers are also a wonderful resource for keeping up with the newest trends. Be nosy. Ask the teens who volunteer in your library what they like and dislike in the library. Get their ideas on how to improve library services to teens.

Many high schools around the country are instituting service requirements for graduation. This is an excellent opportunity to get teens into the library and build relationships with them.

Booktalking

Booktalking is a great way to broaden the horizons of teen readers. Excellent examples of booktalks can be found in The Booktalker series by Joni Richards Bodart, published by Wilson, and in *The New Booktalker* published by Libraries Unlimited. Patrick Jones in *Connecting Young Adults and Libraries* (Neal-Shuman, 1992), provides examples of booktalks and a comprehensive outline of how to plan and execute booktalking programs.

One of the best ways to demonstrate credibility when booktalking to a group of teens is to booktalk a genre book that is wildly popular. Talking about the newest Piers Anthony *Xanth* novel or an R. L. Stine may not introduce anything new to the listeners but it does help establish credibility. If the booktalker knows and likes what the teens like, perhaps some of the other books discussed might be worth taking a look at.

Marketing to Teens

If libraries and bookstores want teen customers, books need to be marketed to teens.

Word of mouth is a teen's main source of information. Teen pages or shelvers who like to read and informally booktalk can increase library use of teen collections dramatically. An enthusiastic recommendation from another teen about a book makes it more desirable.

Because word of mouth is so important in the teen world, sometimes a book will really take off in a specific geographic area because it somehow got hooked into the network of teen readers. One popular middle school student of my acquaintance only reads one or two books a year but she talks about whatever she does like to her friends. This creates real runs on specific titles. When she read *Heartbeat*, by Norma Fox Mazer and Harry Mazer, her public library ended up with a six month long hold list!

Booktalking visits to schools, juvenile correctional facilities, shelters, and other places teens can be found in supervised groups are excellent places to market the library. And of course, by booktalking, one is marketing the specific books. By taking "the show on the road" the booktalker is able to demonstrate the attitudes and resources available at the library.

Teens are likely to take a librarian's or bookseller's recommendations if they are knowledgeable, enthusiastic, and familiar with books that teens like.

LIBRARIES AND
TEEN GENRE FICTION

Book publishing does differ for teens and adults. There are far fewer general fiction novels written for teens than there are books that fit into a particular genre. In fact, some of the best written books for teens fall into genre areas. In 1994, of the 60 fiction titles selected as "Best Books for Young Adults" by the ALA, 37 of them (or 62 percent) could be considered genre titles.

Teen sections vary widely from library to library. Some libraries have well-established and heavily used teen sections. In other libraries a well-stocked and defined teen section does not seem to attract teen readers. Teen sections can be found in Children's or Adult Services areas of libraries. Teens do not like to be regarded as children. Without an exceptional marketing program, teen collections in close proximity to children's sections have a hard time attracting readers. Depending on the community, sometimes even having a defined teen section in adult services will not work. The teen books were not used at all in the Washington County Library, in a small rural southern town. The teens in that community considered themselves adults as far as reading was concerned. When teen novels were intershelved with adult fiction, they suddenly started to circulate.

Libraries deal with the physical aspects of managing genre collections in different ways. The best way of managing them is definitely subjective. The size of the collection plays an important role. According to Sharon Baker, who writes on the subject of reducing information overload for fiction-reading library users, physically separating genre fiction from large collections helps readers find what they want to read. In many libraries the teen collections are very small, so information overload may not present a major problem. Teens who like genre fiction are happy to find what they want to read. Different avenues of identifying genre fiction work for differently sized collections. In large collections separating the genres works well; in smaller collections genre spine labels and booklists may suffice.

Many teens really do judge a book by its cover, which is possibly one of the reasons that paperbacks are so popular. If a book is being selected by its cover it makes sense to display it so that the cover shows. Many manufacturers of library shelving are now producing slanted shelving for face-out display. A good low-cost alternative for paperback collections is videocassette display shelving.

Another excellent way of making genre fiction attractive and enticing to readers is to use "dumps," the stand-alone cardboard displayers used in bookstores. The ALA and Baker and Taylor had a joint project featuring genre fiction where a "dump" or paperback displayer complete with books and bibliography bookmarks could be purchased. Unfortunately, the dumps developed specifically for this are no longer available. A friendly bookseller may be willing to pass on some of these cardboard displayers. Another source is to watch the major book jobbers catalogs for dumps featuring assorted titles. Even though the dumps are usually sold stocked with only one title or perhaps a few titles by a single author, occasionally a dump featuring mixed titles is made available. St. Martin's Press produced one called Women of Mystery that featured a few copies of books by several different women authors complemented by an appropriately sinister looking header or decorative cutout. When the adult mystery section of the library was done with the dump, it made an effective display in the teen area for scary books of suspense. Tor Books is the only publisher (this author knows of) that has produced dumps specifically for the teen market. They have one available that features assorted classics. The cover illustrations range from attractive and enticing to nothing special. The headers seem to apply specifically for use in schools but the dumps can be used without the headers. This is an excellent way to display teen books.

The greatest advantage a teen reader can have is a librarian who really cares that the reader find books with which to connect and who reads and likes teen books.

RESOURCES FOR LIBRARIANS

The Young Adult Library Services Association, a division of the ALA, provides support to librarians working with teens by providing programs at the ALA annual conference, and publishing the annual book lists "*Best Books for Young Adults*" and "*Quick Picks.*" They also offer a registry of speakers who are available to present workshops on young adult library services topics including genre fiction.

TOPICS

Bibliographies

The following bibliographies include books for teens in general, not just genre fiction. In fact most of them even include nonfiction.

Anderson, Vicki. *Fiction Index for Readers 10–16: Subject Access to Over 8200 Books (1960–1990)*. McFarland, 1992.

Bodart, Joni Richards. *One Hundred World Class Thin Books; Or What to Read When Your Book Report Is Due Tomorrow*. Libraries Unlimited, 1993.

Carter, Betty. *Best Books for Young Adults: The Selections, the History, the Romance*. ALA, 1994. Lists and annotates all the titles selected for the Best Books for Young Adults lists from 1966–1992.

Gillespie, John T., and Corinne J. Naden. *Seniorplots: A Book Talk Guide to Use with Readers Ages 15–18*. Bowker, 1986.

Olderr, Steven, and Candace Smith, eds. *Olderr's Young Adult Fiction Index, 1990*. St. James Press, 1991.

Spencer, Pam, ed. *What Do Young Adults Read Next? A Reader's Guide to Fiction for Young Adults*. Gale, 1994. The emphasis is on books for grades 6–12 published between 1988 and 1992.

Young Adult Reader's Advisor, Vol. 1. R. R. Bowker, 1992.

Guides for Working with Teens

Chelton, Mary K., and James M. Rosinia. *Bare Bones: Young Adult Services Tips for Public Library Generalists*. Public Library Association/Young Adult Library Services Association, ALA, 1993.

Directions for Library Service to Young Adults. 2d ed. Young Adult Library Services Association, ALA, 1993.

Jones, Patrick. *Connecting Young Adults and Libraries: A How to Do It Manual*. Neal-Schuman, 1992. An indispensable guide for anyone working in libraries with teens.

Journals

VOYA (*Voice of Youth Advocates*)
Scarecrow Press
P. O. Box 4167
Metuchen, NJ 08840
> In addition to reviews of books of interest to teens, articles on teen genres and programs for teens are included. VOYA does an annual roundup of science fiction, fantasy, and horror titles, selecting the best from what they have reviewed over the past year.

School Library Journal
249 West 17th Street
New York, NY 10011

Carolyn Caywood writes the excellent column "In the Young Adult Corner." From time to time guest columnists are featured. SLJ also frequently publishes articles of interest to librarians working with teens.

Kliatt
33 Bay State Road
Wellesley, MA 02121

Reviews paperbacks and includes occasional short articles and bibliographies useful for working with teens.

JOYS (*Journal Of Youth Services*)
American Library Association
50 East Huron Street
Chicago, IL 60611

Articles, bibliographies, and news for the youth divisions of the ALA.

Online Resources

Online resources that can keep pace with rapid change are an asset in keeping up with teen reading interests. Moving and changing continuously, the volatility of the web sites and listservs that make them so current can also be a drawback. The URL, or web site addresses, and other online resource information included in this book were correct and up-to-date as of October 1996 but are liable to change.

WORLD WIDE WEB

The *Genreflecting Page* provides some reviews of teen genre fiction as well as links to web sites of interest to those involved with genre fiction and teen readers. http://www.oz.net/ica/genre

The *YOUNG ADULT LIBRARIAN'S HELP/HOMEPAGE* edited by Patrick Jones is found on the World Wide Web at http://www.acpl.lib.in.us/young_adult_lib_ass/yaweb.html. It features links to over 200 locations and documents on the information superhighway. The six subject areas covered are: Introduction, Starting Points, Reading Pages, Professional Pages, Teen Pages, and Ending Points. (This information is current as of June 25, 1996.)

The *Adolescent Literature Quick Author List* provides links to pages dealing with authors that are read by teens. http://www.educ.kent.edu:80/personal/ted2/authors.html

LISTSERV

Listservs, sometimes call e-conferences, allow groups to discuss issues by using e-mail for communication.

PUBYAC

PUBYAC is an online group discussion of issues relating to library services for children and young adults.

Subscribe by sending an e-mail message to listserv@nysernet.org. The message text should be: subscribe PUBYAC <Firstname Lastname>.

Historical Novels

I like historical fiction because it stays with me after I've read it and I can cross apply it to my life. (Sometimes I even impress someone.)

—Nancy Strippel, age 15

Historical fiction brings history to life by adding a little spice.

—Chessa Skillo, age 15

Many teens do enjoy historical novels, the adventure and romance of dashing heroes and heroines set in different times. The lure of historical fiction calls out to different kids for many different reasons. Historical fiction is widely different, ranging from regency romances to Native American survival stories. Often historical novels are assigned for school. Even though the following listings may be helpful for that, they are primarily provided to assist teens in finding the stories they want to read. Other sources of listings for historical fiction can be found in the Topics Section of this chapter.

Teen readers who enjoy historical fiction are among the most knowledgeable of teen readers. They often research further the time periods they discover in historical fiction. There is a general consensus among teen historical fiction readers that reading historical fiction has the beneficial side effect of providing them with a good background understanding for history class! This author picked up enough information from reading historical romance to pass eleventh grade American history. Purely from anecdotal evidence, it seems that many writers were teens who read historical fiction. Steven Saylor, author of a popular adult series of mystery novels set in the Roman Empire, has mentioned the influence of reading the We Were There books as a youth.

Tastes in historical fiction vary widely. Recently three fifteen-year-old girls attending a family reunion were asked about their reading preferences. All three stated historical novels were their favorites but what they were reading widely differed. One was reading Bertrice Small's sweet and savage adult romances from the 1970s, another was reading the Gilbert Morris and

Bodie Thoene inspirational historicals, and the third was a big fan of the Ann Rinaldi historical novels written specifically for a teen audience. These readers of historical fiction revealed that even within a category there is wide variety for different tastes.

PREHISTORY

Jean Auel launched a popular new genre in 1980 with *The Clan of the Cave Bear*. Tales of strong youths in prehistory have the appeal of adventure and discovery. The following are some that are enjoyed by teens.

> Auel, Jean. *The Clan of the Cave Bear. The Mammoth Hunters. The Valley of Horses. The Plains of Passage.*
>
> Brennan, J. H. *Shiva. Shiva Accused. Shiva's Challenge.*
>
> Dickinson, Peter. *A Bone from a Dry Sea.*
>
> Gear, W. Michael, and Kathleen O'Neal Gear. *People of the Wolf. People of the Fire. People of the Earth. People of the Lakes. People of the River. People of the Sea.*
>
> Harrison, Sue. *Mother Earth, Father Sky. My Sister the Moon. Brother Wind.*
>
> Jordan, Sherryl. *Wolf-Woman.*
>
> Pryor, Bonnie. *Seth of the Lion People.*

NORTH AMERICA

This section contains historical fiction set throughout North America, not only in the United States. While there are few historical novels set in Mexico or Canada circulating to teens in U.S. libraries, the few that could be found are included.

Westerns

The lure of the west still calls to teen readers. Many male reluctant readers find the joys of reading from picking up Louis L'Amour novels. Westerns are strong, simple adventure stories set in the historical American West of the nineteenth and sometimes, the early twentieth centuries.

TRADITIONAL WESTERNS

The traditional western present a conflict between good and evil. They are strong on action and light on romance. The protagonists tend to be chaste, honorable, and loyal, willing to chance the loss of life or limb to fight for what they believe in or in the interests of people who matter to them. Zane Grey and Louis L'Amour both wrote prolifically, leaving a huge legacy for readers of traditional westerns.

Carter, Peter. *Borderlands.*

Estleman, Loren D. *Sudden Country.*

Grey, Zane.

L'Amour, Louis.

McMurtry, Larry. *Lonesome Dove.*

Mulford, Clarence. *Hopalong Cassidy.*

Portis, Charles. *True Grit.*

Reaver, Chap. *A Little Bit Dead.*

Schaefer, Jack. *Shane.*

HUMOROUS WESTERNS

Encompassing both parody and the picaresque, the following westerns do not necessarily present the "good guys" as heroic.

Karr, Kathleen. *Oh, Those Harper Girls!* The humorous tale of five sisters who try everything from making moonshine, to cattle rustling, and stagecoach robbing to keep the family ranch solvent.

Myers, Walter Dean. *The Righteous Revenge of Artemis Bonner.* Wild tale of Artemis's adventures in the West trying to solve the mystery of his uncle's murder with coyote/roadrunner type action.

ROMANTIC WESTERN

A love interest makes the romantic western appealing to female readers as well as to males. The hero may personify all that is strong and honorable in the western hero or he may be flawed. The outlaw has the "bad boy" appeal but often he has sterling virtues as well. The following were written for adults but are enjoyed by teens.

Bonner, Cindy. *Lily.* A young woman falls in love with a boy who she assumes is harmless but is actually a wanted shootist. In *Looking After Lily*, Haywood, Lily's brother-in-law leaves the outlaw life to look after her and her baby while they await Shot's release from jail.

Dailey, Janet. *This Calder Sky. Calder Range. Stands a Calder Man. Calder Born, Calder Bred. The Pride of Hannah Wade.* The Calder series features several generations of love in a western family.

NATIVE AMERICANS

Native Americans make up a significant proportion of the characters in historical fiction for teens. The titles that follow include stories with Native-American characters from prehistoric times to the early twentieth century.

Bruchac, Joseph. *Dawn Land.* Young Hunter travels to the West with his loyal dog companions to save his people from a supernatural threat.

Burks, Brian. *Runs with Horses.* An Apache youth comes of age as the last band of resisting Apaches concedes defeat.

Carter, Forrest. *The Education of Little Tree.* A boy is raised and educated by his Cherokee grandparents in the rural South in the first part of this century.

Conley, Robert J. *Nickajack.* A hauntingly sad tale of conflicts between the Cherokee after the Trail of Tears.

Garland, Sherry. *Indio.* Ipta is captured by Spaniards and sold into slavery in the silver mines.

George, Jean Craighead. *Julie of the Wolves.* Julie, a Native-American girl, befriends a wolf pack after becoming lost in the Alaskan wilderness.

Hudson, Jan. *Sweetgrass.* A fifteen-year-old Blackfoot girl comes of age as a smallpox epidemic decimates her people.

Hudson, Jan. *Dawn Rider.* Kit Fox secretly learns how to ride a horse; a skill that will allow her to save her people.

James, J. Alison. *Sing for a Gentle Rain.* A modern boy is transported back to live with the Anasazi.

Jones, Douglas C. *Gone the Dreams and the Dancing.*

O'Dell, Scott. *Island of the Blue Dolphins.* A young girl is left alone on an island off the coast of California.

O'Dell, Scott. *Streams to the River, River to the Sea.* Sacagawea's tale of the Lewis and Clark expedition.

Power, Susan. *The Grass Dancer.* A multigenerational tale of a Sioux family.

Spinka, Penina Keen. *White Hare's Horses.* A Chumash girl living in 1520s California frees a small herd of horses from Aztecs who had fled to the North with them.

Thomasma, Kenneth. *Naya Nuki: Girl Who Ran.* A Shoshone girl's story.

Vick, Helen Hughes. *Walker of Time.* A fifteen-year-old Hopi is transported back in time 800 years to when the Sinagua people left their ancient cliff dwellings. His story is continued in *Walker's Journey Home.*

INDIAN CAPTIVES

The stories of Indian captives written for teens usually feature the positive aspects of the captive's lives with a Native-American tribe and the devastation caused by their return to the white world.

Hotze, Sollace. *A Circle Unbroken*. A teen girl is unhappily reunited with her remaining family after being adopted by Indians.

Keehn, Sally M. *I Am Regina*. Captured and taken away from an eighteenth-century Pennsylvania farm at age 11 by Indians, Regina lives her teen years as Tskinnak.

Meyer, Carolyn. *Where the Broken Heart Still Beats*. Story of Cynthia Anne Parker after her return to the white world.

Thom, James Alexander. *Follow the River*. A lengthy trade paperback written for adults about a woman in the seventeenth century captured by Indians who travels an enormous distance to return to her home.

Colonial and Revolutionary Days

The early days of United States history provide an exciting and sometimes thought provoking setting. The American Revolution and the Salem witchcraft trials are two of the most popular themes in historical fiction dealing with this era. While not always remembered, there was a Spanish colonial influence in the Southwest and Florida as well as in Mexico in the early days of the European settlement of North America.

Avi. *The Fighting Ground*. Jonathan joins with the Colonial rebels.

Boyd, James. *Drums*. North Carolinian Johnny Fraser joins in the fight for independence from the British.

Clapp, Patricia. *Witches' Children*. An indentured servant's story of the Salem witchcraft trials.

Collier, James Lincoln, and Christopher Collier. *My Brother Sam Is Dead*. Tim Meeker's thoughts and emotions are divided. His older and much admired brother Sam has joined the American Revolutionary Army but his father remains a staunch supporter of the English King.

Fleischman, Paul. *Saturnalia*. In Massachusetts of the 1680s, William, a Narraganset boy, is apprenticed to a printer.

Forbes, Esther. *Johnny Tremain*. A classic Newbery Award winner.

Garland, Sherry. *Indio*. An Indian girl is taken under the wing of two Spanish padres after she is captured as a slave.

Grey, Zane. American Revolutionary series: *Betty Zane. The Last Trail. Spirit of the Border*.

Jakes, John. *The Bastard*. First book in the Kent Family Chronicles follows the adventures of a young Frenchman in colonial America.

Koller, Jackie French. *The Primrose Way*. A colonial girl finds friendship and romance with the Native Americans.

Marino, Jose Maria. *Dreams of Gold*. The son of a conquistador joins an expedition of exploration.

O'Dell, Scott. *Sarah Bishop*. During the American Revolution, British-born Sarah flees Long Island while New York City burns to take refuge in the wilderness.

Rinaldi, Ann. *A Break with Charity*. The Salem witchcraft trials.

Rinaldi, Ann. *A Ride into Morning*. American Revolution.

Rinaldi, Ann. *The Fifth of March*. The Boston Massacre.

Rinaldi, Ann. *Finishing Becca*. Becca is in service to Peggy Shippen to finish her education, but with Peggy's relationship with Benedict Arnold, Becca's education takes an unexpected turn.

Rinaldi, Ann. *Time Enough for Drums*. Fifteen-year-old Jemima of Trenton, New Jersey, is a member of a family divided between American patriots and Tories. She is a patriot but what would happen if she were to fall in love with her Tory tutor?

Rinaldi, Ann. *The Secret of Sarah Revere*. American Revolution.

Nineteenth Century

The nineteenth century saw enormous social changes including industrialization in the North, the abolition movement, the Civil War, Reconstruction, and westward expansion.

Armstrong, Jennifer. *Steal Away*. An abolitionist northern girl sent to the South to live with relatives becomes friends with the slave given her and they "steal away."

Armstrong, William H. *Sounder*. The coming-of-age tale of the son in a Southern share-cropper family.

Avi. *The True Confessions of Charlotte Doyle*. In 1831, Charlotte Doyle, the only passenger aboard the *Seahawk* is accused of murder, brought to trial, and found guilty.

Charbonneau, Eileen. *In the Time of the Wolves*. Joshua Woods is 14 in 1824, the year without summer that wreaks devastation on his Catskill mountain home.

Collier, James Lincoln, and Christopher Collier. *With Every Drop of Blood*. A Southern boy is the captive of an African American Union soldier, both learning from each other.

Conrad, Pam. *Prairie Songs*. A tale of pioneer life on the Nebraska prairie.

Cooper, J. California. *Family*. An African American family's emergence from slavery.

D'Aguiar, Fred. *The Longest Memory*. Chapel is trying to escape from slavery when he is betrayed.

Fleischman, Paul. *Bull Run*. A series of vignettes about people affected by the Battle of Bull Run.

Forman, James D. *Becca's Story*. Both of Becca's beaus enlist to fight in the Civil War.

Hansen, Joyce. *Which Way Freedom?* A teen joins an African American regiment to fight for freedom.

Holland, Isabelle. *Behind the Lines*. The 1863 New York City Draft Riots.

Hunt, Irene. *Across Five Aprils*. Civil War.

Lasky, Kathryn. *The Bone Wars*. Dinosaur bones are discovered in the 1870s during the Indian Wars.

Levitin, Sonia. *The No-Return Trail*. The way west with seventeen-year-old Nancy Kelsey, a wife and mother.

Lyons, Mary E. *Letters from a Slave Girl*. The fictionalized story of Harriet Jacobs.

Mazzio, Joann. *Leaving Eldorado*. Epistolary novel told by a fourteen-year-old girl in 1890s mining setting.

Mitchell, Margaret. *Gone with the Wind*. This large-scale romance of the Civil War era life of Scarlet O'Hara has captivated female teen readers for generations.

Nixon, Joan Lowery. *High Trail to Danger. A Deadly Promise*. Set in Leadville, Colorado, in 1879. Sarah searches for her missing father then tries to clear his name.

Paterson, Katherine. *Lyddie*. Lyddie follows the path of many young women of the early nineteenth century and becomes a "factory girl." She works in a Lowell, Massachusetts, mill, enduring horrible conditions, in an attempt to save the family farm.

Paulsen, Gary. *Nightjohn*. A man allows himself to be captured as a slave so he can teach the enslaved children to read.

Rinaldi, Ann. *In My Father's House*. Osceola and her family are affected by the Civil War as the first battle of Bull Run erupts on her stepfather's plantation. He moves the family to the Appomatox Courthouse to get them away from the front lines, only to have the final battle also occur on his property.

Rinaldi, Ann. *Last Silk Dress*. Susan contributes to the Confederate war effort by collecting silk dresses to make a balloon for spying on the Yankees.

Rinaldi, Ann. *Wolf by the Ears.* Thomas Jefferson's daughter Harriet Hemmings must discover the importance of freedom. When she turns twenty-one she will be released from slavery and removed from all she has ever known.

Stolz, Mary. *Cezanne Pinto.* Cezanne's escape from slavery followed by life as a cowboy.

Taylor, Theodore. *Walking up a Rainbow.* Susan's inheritance is nearly 2,000 sheep and a huge debt. She sets out to drive the sheep to California from Iowa in the 1880s.

Wisler, G. Clifton. *Red Cap.* A thirteen-year-old Civil War drummer is captured and held in Andersonville prison.

IMMIGRATION

The loss of a familiar home, and the trials, tribulations, adventure, and joy of finding a new home in the New World are all to be found in novels of immigration. The youthful protagonists overcome obstacles during their relocation. Some of the following books are set in the nineteenth century while others are set in the first half of the twentieth century.

Angell, Judie. *One-Way to Ansonia.* Rose Olshansky was 14 when she was married in New York City, only four years after emigrating from Russia.

Conlon-McKenna, Marita. *Wildflower Girl.* Peggy O'Driscoll immigrates to Boston after surviving Ireland's Great Famine.

Hesse, Karen. *Letters from Rifka.* Rifka's experiences as she flees Russia with her family in 1919.

Levitin, Sonia. *Silver Days.* The Platts fled Nazi Germany to take up life in America, first in Brooklyn, then in Southern California.

Lingard, Joan. *Between Two Worlds.* The Petersons, Latvian refugees, settle into life in Toronto following World War II.

Morpurgo, Michael. *Twist of Gold.* A brother and sister searching for their father travel across America with a family heirloom, the only thing they have left of Ireland.

Nixon, Joan Lowery. Ellis Island series: *Land of Hope* and *Land of Promise.*

Twentieth Century

Historical fiction is always changing. What is history depends on one's perception. All contemporary fiction eventually becomes historical fiction, if it stays around long enough. Jane Austen's books were contemporary novels when she wrote them in the early nineteenth century. We now, and throughout this century, have seen them as delightful historicals. To teens, the Civil

Rights movement and the Vietnam War are history. These events happened before they were born.

Curtis, Christopher Paul. *The Watsons Go to Birmingham, 1963.* Civil Rights movement.

French, Albert. *Billy.* Mississippi in the 1930s.

Greene, Bette. *Summer of My German Soldier.* World War II.

Gregory, Kristiana. *Earthquake at Dawn.* The 1906 San Francisco Earthquake.

Hahn, Mary Downing. *Stepping on the Cracks.* World War II.

Jones, Adrienne. *Long Time Passing.* Vietnam War era.

Krisher, Trudy. *Spite Fences.* Civil Rights movement in Georgia.

Meyer, Carolyn. *White Lilacs.* In the 1920s, an African American community in Texas is destroyed to make room for a park.

Montgomery, Lucy Maude. The *Anne of Green Gables* series. Prince Edward Island, Canada, turn of the century.

Myers, Walter Dean. *Fallen Angels.* Ritchie should never have even been in the army but he ends up in the middle of the Vietnam War.

Paterson, Katherine. *Jacob Have I Loved.* World War II era.

Paulsen, Gary. *The Cookcamp.* A young boy is sent to stay with his grandmother, a cook for a Minnesota road building crew in 1944.

Qualey, Marsha. *Come in from the Cold.* Vietnam War era.

Reaver, Chap. *Bill.* Prohibition era in Kentucky.

Rostkowski, Margaret I. *After the Dancing Days.* World War I.

Rylant, Cynthia. *I Had Seen Castles.* World War II.

Savin, Marcia. *The Moon Bridge.* World War II.

Stolz, Mary. *Ivy Larkin.* Great Depression.

Taylor, Mildred D. *Roll of Thunder, Hear My Cry. Let the Circle Be Unbroken. Road to Memphis.* Great Depression.

Thesman, Jean. *Molly Donnelly.* World War II.

White, Ellen E. *The Road Home.* Rebecca returns from serving as a nurse in the Vietnam War.

White, Ruth. *Bell Prater's Boy.* Appalachia in the 1950s.

SAGAS

Not too many sagas have been written for teens. Among those written for adults but enjoyed by teens are the Kent Family Chronicles by John Jakes as well as the romantic sagas by Janette Oke and Bodie Thoene. There is one notable saga written specifically for teens that comes to mind. *The Glory Field* by Walter Dean Myers tells the story of an African American family from earliest days of slavery to the civil rights movement.

EUROPE

Romance in the historical settings of old Europe can conjure up visions of turreted castles, ladies fair, and knights in gleaming armor. When some think of historical Europe or England, the legends of King Arthur and Robin Hood spring to mind. Because of the legendary nature of those characters in early eras they are treated in Chapter 4. While a few of the following historical novels have medieval settings, most are concerned with twentieth century history. A section on World War II and the Holocaust follows this section.

Alder, Elizabeth. *The King's Shadow*. A boy from Wales in the eleventh century.

Cushman, Karen. *The Midwife's Apprentice*. A medieval setting.

Garden, Nancy. *Dove & Sword: A Novel of Joan of Arc*.

Holman, Felice. *The Wild Children*. Russian Revolution.

Lester, Julius. *Othello: A Novel*.

Lingard, Joan. *Sisters by Rite*. Three friends from vastly different religious backgrounds grow into womanhood in Belfast, Ireland between 1944 and 1970.

Lutzeier, Elizabeth. *The Wall*. The fall of the Berlin wall lends a backdrop to a story of coming of age amidst loss and social upheaval.

Matas, Carol. *The Burning Time*. A young woman sees her mother tortured after being accused of witchcraft in sixteenth-century France.

Posell, Elsa. *Homecoming*. Russian Revolution.

Pullman, Philip. *The Tin Princess*. Nineteenth century.

Temple, Frances. *The Ramsay Scallop*. At the end of the thirteenth century, a young couple is sent on a pilgrimage to Spain.

Walsh, Jill Paton. *Grace*. A young woman performs a heroic rescue that forever changes her life.

World War II and the Holocaust

A popular era to write about, more books about World War II and the Holocaust come out every year. The required reading in school of Anne Frank's *The Diary of a Young Girl* is often the catalyst that sparks interest in teen readers.

Garfield, Brian. *The Paladin*. A teenager is recruited by Winston Churchill to be a secret agent in World War II.

Laird, Crista. *But Can the Phoenix Sing?* Jewish resistance in Poland.

Lowry, Lois. *Number the Stars.* A Danish girl in hiding from the Nazis.

Magorian, Michelle. *Back Home.* England in the 1940s.

Magorian, Michelle. *Good Night, Mr. Tom.* An abused child from London is thrust into the care of a reluctant elderly man during World War II.

Mazer, Harry. *The Last Mission.* Fifteen years old and Jewish, Jack Raab lied his way into the U.S. Air Corps only to become a prisoner of the Germans.

Orlev, Uri. *The Man from the Other Side.* Anti-Semitic Marek makes profits in the sewers under the Warsaw ghetto during World War II, then his mother reveals his Jewish ancestry to him.

Reiss, Johanna. *The Upstairs Room.* A farming family in the Netherlands hides two Jewish sisters from the Holocaust.

Reuter, Bjarne. *Boys from St. Petri.* Several young men gradually find themselves fighting the Nazis through sabotage.

Van Dijk, Lutz. *Damned Strong Love.* A gay Polish teen falls in love with a German soldier.

Westall, Robert. *Blitzcat.* The World War II adventures of Lord Gort, a cat.

Westall, Robert. *The Kingdom by the Sea.* When Harry's family is killed in a bombing raid, he sets out with a canine companion and travels the British coast to Lindisfarne.

Westall, Robert. *The Machine Gunners.* Chas McGill and his friends salvage a machine gun from a fallen German plane.

AFRICA AND THE MIDDLE EAST

Berry, James. *Ajeemah and His Son.* The eponymous characters are snatched from Africa in 1807 and sold into slavery in Jamaica.

Gedge, Pauline. *Child of the Morning.* The story of Hatshepsut, the only woman pharaoh.

Levitin, Sonia. *Escape from Egypt.* Two very different friends escape with Moses' Exodus from Egypt.

McGraw, Eloise Jarvis. *Mara, Daughter of the Nile.* Remarkably, this novel, published in 1953, still finds young teen readers.

Orlev, Uri. *Lady with the Hat.* Seventeen-year-old Ulek tries to make a life for himself in Palestine after surviving a Nazi concentration camp.

ASIA AND THE PACIFIC

Bosse, Malcolm. *The Examination.* Two brothers travel through China, one to take the civil service exam, the other to protect and guide him.

Choi, Sook Nyul. *Year of Impossible Goodbyes.* After surviving World War II, a North Korean family must flee the communists. *Echoes of the White Giraffe.* Their life in a refugee camp is chronicled.

Namioka, Lensey. *Island of Ogres. Village of the Vampire Cat. Valley of the Broken Cherry Trees. The Coming of the Bear.* A series of novels featuring two young Samurai in medieval Japan.

Paterson, Katherine. *The Sign of the Chrysanthemum.* Twelfth-century Japan.

Paterson, Katherine. *The Master Puppeteer.* Eighteenth-century Japan.

Salisbury, Graham. *Under the Blood Red Sun.* A Japanese-American boy living in Hawaii experiences first hand the bombing of Pearl Harbor and its aftermath.

Taylor, Theodore. *The Bomb.* After World War II, Sorry Rinamu tries to stop the atomic bomb test that will render his Bikini Island home uninhabitable.

Watkins, Yoko K. *So Far from the Bamboo Grove.* As World War II ends, a Japanese family tries to escape Korea to return to their homeland.

Watkins, Yoko K. *My Brother, My Sister, and I.* The three remaining members of the family face homelessness, suspicion, and accidents in Japan following World War II.

TOPICS

YALSA Historical Fiction Genre List

The following list was compiled by the American Library Association's Young Adult Library Services Association Historical Fiction Genre committee and is reprinted here with permission.

Historical fiction can take young adults to places and times that can be reached no other way. Some of the people they meet will be real, others only imagined. Some of the problems in the stories are still problems in today's world, while some are unique to the time and place of the story. Imagination carries the reader to these people, these times, these places—and the stories make history come alive.

Where the Broken Heart Still Beats. Meyer, Carolyn. Harcourt Brace. 0-15-295602-6. 1992. Paper $6.95. Captured by Indians as a child and accepting their ways, Cynthia Ann Parker must struggle with conflicting cultures when she returns to live with pioneer relatives.

Wolf by the Ears. Rinaldi, Ann. Scholastic. 0-590-43412-8. 1993. Paper $3.50. Harriet Hemmings, believed to be the daughter of Thomas Jefferson, and one of his slaves, Sally Hemmings, faces constant conflict between the black and white worlds.

Summer of the Monkeys. Rawls, Wilson. Bantam. 0-553-29818-6. 1992. Paper $3.99. In the turn-of-the-century Ozarks, Jay Berry and his hound Old Rowdy find catching escaped circus monkeys is not as easy as Grandfather promises.

The Bone Wars. Lasky, Kathryn. Puffin. 0-014-0341684. 1989. Paper $5.99. Thad, a teen scout in the 1870s, finds his destiny linked to three rival teams of paleontologists who search for bones as the Plains Indians prepare for war.

The True Confessions of Charlotte Doyle. Avi. Avon. 0-380-7145-2. 1992. Paper $3.99. Caught in a mutiny at sea, Charlotte Doyle discovers unknown personal strength and abilities. A Newbery Honor Book.

Year of Impossible Goodbyes. Choi, Sook Nyul. Dell 0-440-40759-1. 1991. Paper $3.50. Sookan and her family survive the Japanese occupation of Korea but then must flee to the south to escape further oppression.

Arly. Peck, Robert Newton. Scholastic. 0-590-43469-1. 1992. Paper $2.95. Arly is destined for a life of hardship like his migrant worker father until a determined teacher comes to Shantytown.

Crocodile Burning. Williams, Michael. Puffin. 0-14-036793-4. 1994. Paper $3.00. Seraki, a South African teenager, learn painful lessons about hatred and hope when his musical troupe travels to New York City.

Chain of Fire. Naidoo, Beverly. HarperTrophy. 0-06440468-4. 1989. Paper $3.95. Naledi and her schoolmates discover strength in their resistance to the South African government's attempt to relocate them and their families.

Letters from Rifka. Hesse, Karen. Puffin. 0-14-036391-2. 1993. Paper $3.99. Rifka, a Jewish refugee from Russia in 1919, shares her loneliness and hopes for a new life in America in letters to her cousin.

Ajeemah and His Son. Berry, James. HarperCollins. 0-06-440523-0. 1993. Paper $3.95. Captured and shipped to Jamaica as slaves, Ajeemah and his son Atu respond in different ways to a life of oppression and adversity.

A Circle Unbroken. Hotze, Sollace. Houghton Mifflin. 0-395-59702-1. 1991. Paper $4.95. After living with Sioux Indians for seven years, teenage Rachel Porter must face prejudice and misunderstanding when she is restored to her family in 1845.

Cold Sassy Tree. Burns, Olive Ann. Dell. 0-440-51442-8. 1986. Paper $12.00. Fourteen-year-old Will Tweedy tells what happens in the little town of Cold Sassy, Georgia, in 1906 when his Grandpa scandalously marries a young woman only three weeks after his first wife's death.

A Place Called Sweet Shrub. Wood, Jane Roberts. Dell. 0-440-50305-1. 1991 Paper $10.00. Lucy Richards arrives in Sweet Shrub, Arkansas, during World War I to find a town simmering with racial unrest.

Prairie Songs. Conrad, Pam. HarperTrophy. 0-06-440206-1. 1987. Paper $3.95. Louisa and her pioneer family discover that life on the Nebraska prairie can be both horrible and beautiful.

Copper Crown. Von Herzen, Lane. Plume. 0-452-26916-4. 1992. Paper $9.00. Cass and Allie reach across the barriers of racism to forge a friendship in a Texas town in 1913.

Shiva: An Adventure in the Ice Age. Brennan, J. H. HarperTrophy. 0-06-440392-0. 1992. Paper $3.95. A Cro-Magnon girl named Shiva befriends an "ogre" boy of the Neanderthals, while their tribes prepare for war.

The Ruby in the Smoke. Pullman, Philip. Knopf. 0-394-89589-4. 1988. Paper $3.99. The death of her father and the theft of a priceless ruby are twin mysteries which challenge sixteen-year-old Sally Lockhart in Victorian England.

The Return. Levitin, Sonia. Fawcett. 0-449-70280-4. 1988. Paper $3.99. Desta is one of 8,000 Ethiopian Jews who is secretly airlifted to Jerusalem in "Operation Moses."

Kindred. 2d ed. Butler, Octavia E. Beacon Press. 0-8-70-8305-4. 1988. Paper $11.95. A young black woman is abruptly transported through time to save the life of the reckless young son of a plantation owner.

YALSA Historical Fiction Genre Committee: Carlos Najera, chair; Sue Davis, Cedar Falls, IA; Elizabeth Elam, Hyattsville, MD; Matthew Laxton, Marysville, WA; Elaine M. McGuire, Findlay, OH; Linda Wilson, Radford, VA; Nancy Bard, Alexandria, VA.

Classics as Historical Fiction

Many classic works of literature can be read and enjoyed as historical fiction. The recent popularity of movies based on the works of James Fenimore Cooper, Jane Austen, and the like demonstrate the continued popularity of the novels. Several also fall into the adventure category.

Alcott, Louisa May. *Little Women*.

Austen, Jane. *Emma. Pride and Prejudice. Sense and Sensibility*.

Brönte, Charlotte. *Jane Eyre*.

Brönte, Emily. *Wuthering Heights*.

Buck, Pearl S. *The Good Earth*.

Cather, Willa. *Death Comes for the Archbishop. My Antonia*.

Cervantes Saavedra, Miguel de. *Don Quixote.*

Chaucer, Geoffrey. *The Canterbury Tales.*

Clark, Walter V. *The Ox-Bow Incident.*

Collins, Wilkie. *The Moonstone.*

Cooper, James Fenimore. *The Last of the Mohicans.*

Crane, Stephen. *The Red Badge of Courage.*

Defoe, Daniel. *Robinson Crusoe.*

Dickens, Charles. *Bleak House. A Tale of Two Cities. Great Expectations.*

Dumas, Alexandre. *The Count of Monte Cristo. The Three Musketeers.*

Du Maurier, Daphne. *Rebecca.*

Eliot, George. *Silas Marner.*

Ferber, Edna. *Cimarron.*

Graves, Robert. *I, Claudius.*

Hardy, Thomas. *Tess of the D'Urbervilles.*

Hawthorne, Nathaniel. *The House of Seven Gables. The Scarlet Letter.*

Hugo, Victor. *The Hunchback of Notre Dame. Les Miserables.*

Kipling, Rudyard. *Kim.*

Lee, Harper. *To Kill a Mockingbird.*

London, Jack. *Sea Wolf.*

Orczy, Baroness Emma. *The Scarlet Pimpernel.*

Pasternak, Boris. *Doctor Zhivago.*

Rawlings, Marjorie Kinnon. *The Yearling.*

Remarque, Erich. *All Quiet on the Western Front.*

Renault, Mary. *The King Must Die.*

Schaefer, Jack. *Shane.*

Steinbeck, John. *The Pearl. Tortilla Flat. The Grapes of Wrath. East of Eden. Of Mice and Men.*

Stowe, Harriet Beecher. *Uncle Tom's Cabin.*

Twain, Mark. *The Adventures of Huckleberry Finn. The Adventures of Tom Sawyer. A Connecticut Yankee in King Arthur's Court.*

Verne, Jules. *Around the World in Eighty Days.*

White, T. H. *The Once and Future King.*

Wister, Owen. *The Virginian.*

Bibliographies

Adamson, Lynda G. *Historical Fiction for Children & Young Adults: An Annotated Bibliography of American and International Titles.* Greenwood Press, 1994.

Fisher, Janet, comp. *An Index to Historical Fiction for Children & Young People.* Ashgate Publishing, 1994. Four hundred sixty-one plot summaries arranged by author, mostly British.

Gerhardstein, Virginia Brokaw, ed. *Dickinson's American Historical Fiction.* 5th ed. Scarecrow, 1986.

Logasa, Hannah. *Historical Fiction.* McKinley, 1964.

D's Picks

Childress, Mark. *Crazy in Alabama.*

Cushman, Karen. *Catherine, Called Birdy.*

Gee, Maurice. *The Champion.*

Lasky, Kathryn. *Beyond the Burning Time.*

Power, Susan. *The Grass Dancer.*

Science Fiction

SF gives me something to ponder when I'm stuck in a boring class.
—Nancy Strippel, age 15

I like to read science fiction because it allows you to explore new worlds and the authors tend to be very creative.
—Kristin Dreves, age 14

Science fiction expands my creativity and my thinking.
—Samuel Baker, age 12

Science fiction and fantasy readers do not stick to "age appropriate" books. Adult readers of those genres can often be found reading science fiction and fantasy from the teen section. Teen readers have no compunctions whatsoever about reading from the adult collection. The books listed here are ones that have been particularly popular with teens, but almost all the titles listed in *Genreflecting: A Guide to Reading Interests in Genre Fiction*, 4th ed. (Libraries Unlimited, 1995) in the science fiction and fantasy chapters will find a readership among the teen fans of the genres. I have attempted to list science fiction published specifically for teens.

How to differentiate between fantasy and science fiction is a frequently debated question. Because the readers, writers, and publishers of SF (the accepted nickname of the genre) and fantasy all tend to have strong opinions on where a particular work fits, there is never going to be any one good way of making the distinction. Querying the authors sometimes brings surprising results.

Dragons, could be thought to fall into the fantasy realm. Anne McCaffrey, best-selling author of the Pern series, emphatically claims that her dragons have a scientific basis so her works dealing with the dragons of Pern are SF rather than fantasy. Many of her fans disagree. Orson Scott Card, Nebula and Hugo award winning author, claims that because his knowledge of science is minimal, and his stories come from his imagination, they are works of fantasy. He has said that you can tell the genre by the book's cover, rivets in the cover illustration denote SF, while foliage denotes fantasy. Some consider SF to be a subgenre of fantasy and others consider fantasy to be a subgenre of SF.

I have categorized the following books based on my personal opinion of where things fit. As no two people ever seem to agree on the delineation, this seems to be the expedient way. Science fiction readers will want to check the fantasy section, and fantasy readers will want to check the science fiction section.

IMHO (Internet-derived acronym for "in my humble opinion") science fiction novels are those that deal with scientific topics, space travel, alien beings, and recognizable variants of our world or species that have not been touched by magic. Time travel not occasioned by magic is here, as are stories of distant civilizations many years in the future that still show a relationship to our universe.

HUMOROUS SCIENCE FICTION

Douglas Adams is possibly the most well-known writer of humorous science fiction. The silliness of his "increasingly misnamed trilogy" of five titles (as of 1994) is just plain good fun. The Hitchhiker's "trilogy" has been a television series and also a very successful audio production. Science fiction readers tend to read voraciously, and as a result many have a wide knowledge of the genre, making "in jokes" practicable.

Adams, Douglas. *Hitchhiker's Guide to the Galaxy. The Restaurant at the End of the Universe. So Long and Thanks for All the Fish. Mostly Harmless.* The continuing adventures of Arthur Dent and Ford Prefect through space and time. *Dirk Gently's Holistic Detective Agency. Long Dark Teatime of the Soul.* A series that stretches the barriers of time and space through unique detecting methods.

Danziger, Paula. *This Place Has No Atmosphere.* A typical teen of the twenty-first century and life on a moon colony.

Gilden, Mel. *The Planetoid of Amazement. The Pumpkins of Time.* Comedic delights for the younger end of the young adult spectrum. *Hawaiian U.F.O. Alien. Surfing Samurai Robots.* Will tickle the funny bones of older teen readers.

Pinkwater, Daniel. *Borgel.* A quest for the cosmic Great Popsicle leads to adventures in space and time.

Robinson, Spider. *Callahan's Crosstime Saloon.* Anyone can and does show up at Callahan's.

ALTERNATE WORLDS

Alternate worlds exist on some dimension parallel to our own. This premise is used in both SF and fantasy. Explainable, nonmagical means of moving from one world to another are included here. Worlds that may have been similar to ours in their distant history are included here. More will be found in Chapter 4.

Some tales are set so far in the future that the setting is more like an alternate world than the worlds in hard SF.

Anthony, Piers. *Virtual Mode. Fractal Mode. Chaos Mode.* Travel through parallel worlds.

Askounis, Christain. *The Dream of the Stone.* After Sarah's parents are killed and her brother, who works for a mysterious organization disappears, she teams up with Angel, a gypsy, and is transported to another world.

Charnas, Suzy McKee. *The Kingdom of Kevin Malone.* A terrifying alternate world lies on the other side of the park's arches.

DeWeese, Gene. *Whatever Became of Aunt Margaret?* David, Julie, and Aunt Margaret try to foil an alien plot.

Jones, Diana Wynne. *A Sudden Wild Magic.* The magicians of Urth inflict their problems on Earth so they can learn how the witches of England would remedy them.

L'Engle, Madeleine. *A Wrinkle in Time.* A classic tale of travel through the dimensions to fight evil.

Lawrence, Louise. *Keeper of the Universe.* Snatched from an exploding airplane, seventeen-year-old Christopher tries to make sense of a universe overseen by galactic controllers.

Levy, Robert. *Escape from Exile.* Inexplicably transported to another world, Daniel discovers he can communicate with some rather unusual animals.

Wilson, Robert Charles. *Mysterium.* The entire town of Two Rivers is zapped into a parallel universe where teens are hanged for violating curfew.

Zelazny, Roger. *A Dark Traveling.* Aliens from a parallel world are waging war against Earth.

ALTERNATE HISTORY

If one little thing in history was changed it could alter the entire future of the world as we know it.

Bova, Ben. *Triumph.* What course would history have taken if President Roosevelt had not died during World War II and had entered into a secret plan to assassinate Stalin?

Dick, Philip K. *Man in the High Castle.* A different world diverging from when the Allied Forces lost World War II.

Card, Orson Scott. The Chronicles of Alvin Maker: *Seventh Son, Red Prophet, 'Prentice Alvin,* and *Alvin Journeyman.* An ongoing series set in a nineteenth-century America where small spells and hexes do work.

Gibson, William, and Bruce Sterling. *The Difference Engine*. In an alternate nineteenth century a steam-powered computer is invented. This novel is sometimes called "steampunk."

Roberts, Keith. *Pavane*. The victory by the Spanish Armada marks the divergence in time.

Turtledove, Harry. The Worldwar series: *In the Balance*. *Tilting the Balance*. An Alien invasion during World War II changes the course of history.

Turtledove, Harry. *Guns of the South*. The South is given advanced weapons by time travelers during the Civil War.

TIME TRAVEL

Traveling through time is a popular device to take characters to exotic settings or untimely conflict; sometimes time travel is merely a segue for a historical novel. The stories found here use some scientific or pseudoscientific ploy to explain the mechanics of time travel. Novels that do not give a "scientific" or mechanical explanation of time travel appear in Chapter 4.

The following were written for adults. It seems that most time travel novels written for teens are fantasy rather than science fiction.

Appel, Allen. *Time After Time*. *Twice Upon a Time*. *Till the End of Time*. Historian Alex Balfour has no control over the eras he will be transported to by his historical research.

Grimwood, Ken. *Replay*. The hero relives his life over and over again, never forgetting his previous lives.

Mason, Connie. *Summer of Love*. Chiron Cat's Eye in Draco travels from the twenty-fifth century back in time to 1967 San Francisco to protect the future.

Varley, John. *Millennium*. Travelers from a dying future travel back in time to rescue people seconds before they would die in disasters to populate the future.

Willis, Connie. *The Doomsday Book*. Plagues in the fourteenth and twenty-first centuries interfere with the life of a young medieval scholar.

PSIONIC POWERS

The possession of paranormal powers is an enticing subject. Psionic powers can include telepathy, or the power to communicate mind to mind; teleportation, or the ability for the mind to transport the body from place to place; telekinesis, or the ability to mentally move objects; and precognition, or the ability to see the future. Psionic powers appear in fantasy and horror novels as well as in SF.

Ashwell, Pauline. *Project Farcry*. A new branch of service is created after it is discovered that a boy has telepathic powers that allow him to communicate with aliens.

Bradley, Marion Zimmer. Darkover series. On a distant planet in a distant time, people communicate by means of *laren*, a telepathic power. This series is SF even though several of the books in the series appear to be fantasy. More recent books in the series clarify that the planet was, in essence, a lost colony of earth. In *Rediscovery*, Earth rediscovers this lost pocket of humanity.

Carmody, Isobelle. *Obernewtyn. The Farseekers. Scatterlings*. Psionic powers help the heroines succeed in a post-holocaust world

Cormier, Robert. *Fade*. Is Paul's inherited ability to disappear at will a gift or a curse?

Farmer, Nancy. *The Ear, the Eye and the Arm*. In Zimbabwe of 2194, three detectives with unusual abilities search for the three missing children of General Matasika.

King, Stephen. *Firestarter*. The government is after a girl, the daughter of psionically talented parents who were the subjects of experiments that may have given her the power to start fires with her mind.

McCaffrey, Anne. *To Ride Pegasus. Get Off the Unicorn. Pegasus in Flight. The Rowan. Damia. Damia's Children. Lyon's Pride*. Characters who have the powers of telekinesis and telepathy.

Schmitz, James H. *The Universe Against Her. The Telzy Toy. The Lion Game*. All feature Telzy Amberdon, a teenage telepath.

Schmitz, James H. *The Witches of Karres*. A space captain rescues three psionically talented girls.

Shusterman, Neal. *The Scorpion Shards*. Six teens have powers they cannot control that are ruining their lives until the six are mysteriously drawn together.

Vinge, Joan D. *Catspaw. Psion*. A telepathic teen tries to survive in the twenty-fifth century.

Wilson, Robert Charles. *Gypsies*. A family with unique powers is on the run through different dimensions.

HARD SCIENCE FICTION

Space exploration and scientific discovery are the two major components of hard SF. Sometimes hard SF is the subgenre that is thought of as defining science fiction. This category includes stories set on other planets settled by humans from Earth, space travel, and other conceivable situations in the not-too-extremely-distant future.

Written for Teens—
Enjoyed by Adults (and Teens!)

Ames, Mildred. *Anna to the Infinite Power*. Clones are being systematically wiped out.

Dickinson, Peter. *Eva*. After a terrible accident, Eva finds that she now resides in the body of a chimpanzee.

Heinlein, Robert A. *Citizen of the Galaxy. Have Space Suit—Will Travel. Starman Jones. The Star Beast*. Classic science fiction adventures written in the 1950s.

Sleator, William. *Singularity*. While peril heads for the Earth, twins find a small building where time moves at a different rate.

Sleator, William. *Interstellar Pig*. The new neighbors at the summer cottage have a game to play that puts the future of our world at stake.

Sleator, William. *The Boy Who Reversed Himself*. Life can turn one inside out when one travels into different dimensions.

Sleator, William. *The Duplicate*. Finding a strange box on the beach, a boy duplicates himself, creating his own evil twin.

Sleator, William. *Strange Attractors*. Time travel leaves a parallel universe in chaos.

Sleator, William. *Others See Us*. Toxic sludge opens up psionic powers.

Written for Adults—Enjoyed by Teens

Asimov, Isaac. *Nightfall*.

Benford, Gregory. *Timescape*.

Bova, Ben. *Mars*.

Brin, David. *Earth*.

Clarke, Arthur C. *Rendezvous with Rama. Fountains of Paradise*.

Crichton, Michael. *Jurassic Park*.

Niven, Larry. *Ringworld*.

SPACE OPERA
AND GALACTIC EMPIRES

Much maligned, space opera is in truth a great deal of fun. Sometimes called westerns in space, they feature almost everything one could want in a story: action, adventure, intrigue, and romance. They often take place in galaxy-spanning empires. The *Star Wars* movie series from George Lucas is an excellent example of space opera. There is some truly great writing turning up in space opera, and novels in this subgenre have been winning respected awards.

Bujold, Lois McMaster. *Shards of Honor. The Warrior's Apprentice. Brothers in Arms. The Vor Game. Barrayar. Mirror Dance. Cetaganda. Memory.* The continuing saga of the militaristic Vorkosigan family featuring Miles, a great military leader despite multiple handicaps.

Cherryh, C. J. *Downbelow Station.* Award-winning SF set on a politically warring space station.

Crispin, A. C. and others write the Starbridge Series which features teen characters at a space academy.

Hill, Douglas. *Galactic Warlord. Deathwing over Beynaa. Day of the Starwind. Planet of the Warlord. Young Legionary.* Keill Rando attempts to avenge the destruction of his world and stop an evil warlord from conquering the universe.

King, Stephen. *The Gunfighter. The Drawing of the Three. The Dark Tower.* A very dark space opera from the king of horror fiction.

McCaffrey, Anne, and Elizabeth Moon. *Sassinak.* Sassinak is kidnapped by pirates at age 12 only to go on to become a space fleet commander.

McCaffrey, Anne, and Elizabeth Ann Scarborough. *Powers That Be.* Retired because of lung damage incurred in the line of duty, Major Yanaba Maddock is asked to spy on her new friends and neighbors on a planet hiding many secrets. *Power Lines* continues her story.

Weis, Margaret. The Star of the Guardians series: *The Lost King, The King's Test,* and *The King's Sacrifice.* Dion Starfire is the heir to a galactic empire that has been overtaken by an evil usurper.

Zahn, Timothy. *Dark Force Rising. Heir to the Empire.* A trilogy of books set a short time after the *Star Wars* films.

MILITARISTIC

Space opera often includes aspects of militaristic science fiction. Militaristic science fiction does not concentrate as heavily on the sociological and political issues found in space opera. The following novels focus on war and warriors in future conflicts. Most are serious, but some militaristic books are also comedic. Turtledove's series features a Roman legion plucked out of time to fight in another place.

Asprin, Robert. *Phule's Company. Phule's Paradise.* Captain Willard Phule turns a company of Space Legion misfits into a disciplined military outfit. Comedy.

Card, Orson Scott. *Ender's Game.* Ender Wiggins is recruited at age six for Battle School where Earth hopes to find a way to defeat the alien Buggers.

Dickson, Gordon R. *Soldier, Ask Not.* The Dorsai are genetically programmed to be soldiers.

Feintuch, David. *Midshipman's Hope.* A seventeen-year-old midshipman is left in command after a series of accidents leaves him the ranking officer.

Haldeman, Joe. *The Forever War.* Private Mandella is forever alienated from an Earth where scores of years pass as he travels the interstellar byways to fight aliens.

Heinlein, Robert A. *Starship Troopers.* In this tale of interstellar war, a young man is transformed into a professional soldier.

Hill, Douglas. *Colsec Rebellion. The Caves of Klydor. Exiles of Colsec.* Young humans survive shipwreck on an alien planet.

Turtledove, Harry. The Videssos Cycle: *The Misplaced Legion, An Emperor for the Legion, Legion of Videssos,* and *Swords of the Legion.* A Roman legion is transported to a space empire to work as mercenaries.

CYBERPUNK

A bleak future where tentacles of technology invade almost everything. The movie *Bladerunner,* based on the novel *Do Androids Dream of Electric Sheep?* by Philip K. Dick is a graphic demonstration of this subgenre.

Cadigan, Pat. *Fools.*

Gibson, William. *Neuromancer. Count Zero. Mona Lisa Overdrive.* Possibly the best known cyberpunk novels, they are graphic and gritty.

Mason, Lisa. *Arachne.* Postearthquake San Francisco.

Stephenson, Neal. *Snow Crash.* Pizza deliverer and creator of a virtual reality world, Hiro Protagonist is faced with fighting a virus both in and out of the Metaverse.

Sterling, Bruce. *Islands in the Net.*

ALIENS

Alien beings and humankind's first contact with them is a staple SF theme. The challenge is in imagining the aliens truly alien enough while providing, at the same time, enough characterization and humanity to connect with the reader.

Ashwell, Pauline. *Project Farcry.* It takes a telepathic boy to discover the aliens on a newly explored planet.

Bear, Greg. *The Forge of God.* Aliens destroy the Earth. *Anvil of Stars.* Teenage survivors of Earth's destruction are on a mission of vengeance.

Brizzolara, John. *Empire's Horizon.*

DeChancie, John. *Living with Aliens.* Comedic story of what happens when two aliens (who look like Danny DeVito) move in with twelve-year-old Drew's family.

Dereske, Jo. *The Lone Sentinel.* Erik remains at Lone Sentinel safeguarding the fields after his father dies, with only a dog for company.

Jacobs, Paul Samuel. *Born into the Light.* Strange feral children are discovered in the woods.

Lindholm, Megan. *Alien Earth.* Humans have been banned from Earth and travel on sentient beastships with whom they cannot communicate.

Sleator, William. *Interstellar Pig.* The neighbors are aliens!

Tepper, Sheri S. *Grass.* On an alien planet a woman finds that there are aliens who take an unexpected form.

Wilder, Cherry. The Torin series: *The Luck of Brin's Five, The Nearest Fire, The Tapestry Warriors.* Young humans become involved with the marsupial inhabitants of the planet.

UTOPIA/DYSTOPIA

Butler, Octavia E. *Parable of the Sower.* Set in the near future when people have retreated behind walled enclaves. Lauren, an empathic young woman, leads others out of the ruins of Los Angeles.

Lawrence, Louise. *The Patchwork People.* In a near-future Wales, impoverished Hugh meets Helena, one of the "privileged few."

Lowry, Lois. *The Giver.* A society where everything is the same, everyone is equal, and all receive the same treatment may not be a great as it seems.

Thompson, Julian. *Gypsyworld.* A pristine world where unwanted and kidnapped teens are taken to start a new life.

POST-APOCALYPSE

The environment gone wrong is the setting for books dealing with survival by teens in the bleak future. Sometimes the cause is pervasive drought, pollution, or plain old atomic fallout.

Baird, Thomas. *Smart Rats.* An extreme remedy for overpopulation.

Blackwood, Gary. *The Dying Sun.* In a new Ice Age, one can either burn up in the overcrowded conditions of northern Mexico or freeze in the glaciers.

Brin, David. *The Postman.* After the end of our current civilization, recovery starts with the donning of a postal uniform.

Hughes, Monica. *The Crystal Drop.* A sister and brother set out from their dead, arid farm in Canada to find someplace they can survive.

Lawrence, Louise. *Children of the Dust.* Descendants of a family that survived a nuclear holocaust.

Maguire, Gregory. *I Feel Like the Morning Star.* Far in the future, dreams visit a young man that lead him to believe that there may be more to the world than his underground survivalist community.

Murphy, Pat. *The City, Not Long After.* The arts are revived in a post-holocaust San Francisco.

O'Brien, Robert C. *Z for Zachariah.* Sixteen-year-old Ann searches for other survivors of a nuclear holocaust after she finds out she is not the last living person.

Oppel, Kenneth. *Dead Water Zone.* Looking for his runaway handi-capped brother, Paul discovers that polluted water may be causing drastic changes in people.

Pace, Sue. *The Last Oasis.* Fleeing the authorities and the safety of the Mall, two teens try to escape to Idaho, where they think they will find water and growing things.

Palmer, David R. *Emergence.* The lone survivor of a bionuclear war.

Stevermer, Caroline. *River Rats.* A paddlewheel plies the polluted and deadly Mississippi, crewed by teens who deliver the mail and rock-and-roll concerts.

Ure, Jean. *Plague.* Returning home after a camping trip, Fran must fight for survival in a plague-devastated world.

VIRTUAL REALITY

Virtual reality is rapidly permeating the SF scene. It is a cross between computers and alternate realities where people are sucked into situations within a computer-created word. A clever variation is the fantasy novel *Witch and Wombat* by Carolyn Cushman in which the characters believe they are playing the ultimate virtual reality game while in reality they are questing through a magical world.

Cross, Gillian. *New World.* Miriam and Stewart find danger when testing a new virtual reality game.

Friesner, Esther. *The Sherwood Game.* A computer nerd brings Robin Hood to life while working on a game that escapes into our world.

Rubinstein, Gillian. *Skymaze.* Players are pitted against their own deepest fears.

Scott, Michael. *Gemini Game*. Fifteen-year-old twins go on the run when the virtual reality game they programmed is blamed for causing irreversible comas in a dozen players.

Stephenson, Neal. *Snow Crash*. Hiro Protagonist is the creator of a popular world that is suddenly infected by a virus.

SHARED WORLDS

Shared world SF stories are taken from many sources. Some started as collaborative efforts by groups of people who wanted to write together, but most frequently they are based on role playing games, video games, or television series. The quality varies widely, some shared world books are formulaic drek but others are finely crafted novels that can stand alone. While some shared worlds started as collaborative efforts, such as the Trillium series by Julian May, Andre Norton, and Marion Zimmer Bradley, others started as an individual novel or series that so captivated readers and writers that more books were written set in the fully created world.

Book-Based Series

This is by no means a comprehensive list. It shows examples only.

Witch World series based on the world created by Andre Norton.

Shell People series based on the world created by Anne McCaffrey.

Darkover series based on the world created by Marion Zimmer Bradley.

Game-Based Series

The worlds that are the settings for the following started out in the realm of role playing games.

Shadowrun. Cyberpunk.

Battletech. Space opera.

Television- and Movie-Based Series

A television series that ran for a couple of seasons in the 1960s has sure had an impact on the world of SF. Star Trek spawned three more TV series, Star Trek: The Next Generation, Deep Space 9, and Voyager, and books, books, and more books have been produced. Some of the greatest SF writers around have taken up their pens to add to the ever growing canon of Star Trek lore. The Star Trek world has not been ignored by librarians either, *Uhura's Song* by Janet Kagan was included on the first science fiction ALA genre list, back in the days when YALSA was YASD.

One of the hardest parts of keeping Star Trek in libraries is the plethora of authors, titles, and series.

Star Trek

Star Trek: The Next Generation

Star Trek: Deep Space 9

Star Trek: Voyager

The long running British television series *Doctor Who* is also a successful book series.

The *Star Wars* movies have also been a source of inspiration for shared world novels.

TOPICS

Reference Resources

Clute, John. *Science Fiction: A Visual Encyclopedia.* Dorling-Kindersly, 1995. Misnamed, this entertaining volume provides a history of the development of several different science fiction media. This works better as a browsing book than for looking up specifics. The time-lines and photos are exceptional.

Clute, John, and Peter Nicholls, eds. *The Encyclopedia of Science Fiction.* St. Martin's Press, 1995. A comprehensive volume of nearly 1,400 pages identifying authors and themes in science fiction. The indispensable SF reference.

Journals

Locus is the news source of the SF world. In addition to reviews, *Locus* reports on the lives of people in the SF world, prints author interviews, provided a conference calendar, and lists all SF, fantasy, and horror released in a specific time period.

VOYA is an excellent source for reviews of SF for teens.

Online SF Resources

The newsgroup "rec.arts.sf.written" can be accessed by using a news-reader on the Internet. It offers an opportunity to participate in discussion of written SF.

Science fiction readers are a major presence on the Internet. There are many sites on the World Wide Web that provide links to SF information. Many SF authors have home pages and frequently post exerpts and short stories. The major publishers of SF also have home pages where information on new books and on authors will be found. *Science Fiction Weekly* on the World Wide Web at http://www.scifi.com/sfw/ is published online.

SF BIBLIOGRAPHY PAGES

Internet Speculative Fiction DataBase http://cu:online.com/~avonruff/sfdbase.html

Science Fiction Resource Guide file://sflovers.rutgers.edu/pub/sf-lovers/Web/sf-resource.guide.html

Yahoo - Arts: Literature: Science Fiction, Fantasy, Horror: Authors http://www.yahoo.com/Arts/Literature/General Science_Fiction__Fantasy__Horror/Authors/

SF PUBLISHERS HOME PAGES

Baen Books Home Page http://www.baen.com/

Spectra Science Fiction http://www.bdd.com/forum/bddforum.cgi/scifi/

Del Rey Homepage http://www.randomhouse.com/delrey/

Warner Aspect http://pathfinder.com/@@TO9++QUARynR4snT/twep/Aspect/Aspect.html

Tor SF and Fantasy http://www.tor.com/

YALSA Science Fiction Genre List

In a world characterized by fast-changing technology and threats to our environment, it's no wonder young people like to read science fiction. Science fiction supplies young readers with answers to their confusing world through speculative stories in which people their own age often become heroes and heroines. These stories, usually focused on the eternal struggle between good and evil, place a major emphasis on human survival. While subjects like global catastrophe can make some science fiction seem very serious and pessimistic, the theme of hope is ever-present.

The Doomsday Book. Willis, Connie. Bantam. 0-553-36273-8. 1993. Paper $5.99. Something goes horribly wrong when history student Kivrin is sent back from the twenty-first century to the Middle Ages.

Project Pendulum. Silverberg, Robert. Bantam. 0-553-28001-5. 1989. Paper $3.95. Twins become involved in an intriguing experiment in time travel.

This Place Has No Atmosphere. Danziger, Paula. Dell. 0-440-40205-0. 1989. Paper $3.50. It's 2057 and life on Earth seems perfect for fifteen-year old Paula—until she learns her family is moving to a colony on the moon.

Starbridge. Crispin, A. C. Ace. 0-441-78329-5. 1989. Paper $4.50. Though Earth's first contact with an alien race starts out well, it soon erupts into violence.

Dream Park. Niven, Larry, and Steven Barnes. Ace. 0-441-16730-6. 1982. Paper $5.50. Which player sneaked out of the fantasy park's South Sea Island game simulation to kill a security guard?

Invitation to the Game. Hughes, Monica. Simon & Schuster. 0-671-86692-3. 1993. Paper $3.95. In 2154 Lisse and her friends find an intriguing opportunity to escape their boredom by playing "The Game."

Exiles of Colsec. Hill, Douglas. Bantam 0-553-27233-0. 1986. Paper $2.95. Exiled from Earth, five young rebels must band together against savage aliens and an even more deadly peril from their home planet.

Plague. Ure, Jean. Puffin. 0-14-036283-5. 1993. Paper $3.99. Three London teens band together to survive when a deadly plague erupts in the wake of nuclear devastation.

Enchantress from the Stars. Engdahl, Sylvia. Collier Bks. 0-02-043031-0. 1989. Paper $3.95. A girl stows away on an interplanetary mission and winds up playing an unexpected role.

Anvil of Stars. Bear, Greg. Warner Books. 0-446-36403-7. 1993. Paper $5.99. Planet Earth is dead, and a troop of "lost boys" and "Wendys" track the planet-killers across the galaxy to a life-and-death showdown.

Skymaze. Rubinstein, Gillian. Pocket Books. 0-671-769-88-X. 1993. Paper $2.99. Teens explore a video game maze that suddenly becomes dangerously real.

Crystal Singer. McCaffrey, Anne. Del Rey/Ballantine. 0-345-38491-1. 1993. Paper $5.99. Would-be concert singer Killashandra Ree, penniless and frustrated, escapes to a world where her musical talent proves valuable.

More Whatdunits, vol. 2. Resnick, Mike, ed. DAW Books. 0-88677-557-4. 1993. Paper $5.00. A surprising collection of science fiction stories with mysterious twists.

The Ugly Little Boy. Asimov, Isaac and Robert Silverberg. Bantam. 0-553-56122-7. 1993. Paper $5.99. A Neanderthal boy is transported to the twenty-first century.

The Dog Wizard. Hambly, Barbara. Del Rey/Ballantine. 0-345-3774-1. 1992. Paper $4.99. Someone is using circles of power to keep a gate to another universe open.

The Dark Beyond the Stars. Robinson, Frank M. Tor. 0-8125-1383-5. 1992. Paper $4.99. A searcher for alien life, Sparrow, at 17, doesn't understand his importance to his home ship, *Astron*.

Gypsyworld. Thompson, Julian. Puffin. 0-14-036531-1. 1993. Paper $3.99. Kidnapped teens are transported to Gypsyworld, a utopia where the environment is treasured and preserved.

Snow Crash. Stephenson, Neal. Bantam. 0-553-56261-4. 1993. Paper $5.99. A pizza deliverer named Hiro Protagonist searches the Metaverse for a villain who has unleashed a deadly computer virus.

Voyagers. Bova, Ben. Tor. 9-8125-0076-8. 1989. Paper $4.95. American and Russian experts search for the meaning behind mysterious radio signals emanating from outer space.

Orvis. Hoover, H. M. Puffin. 0-14-032113-6. 1990. Paper $3.95. Two teens risk their lives to rescue an obsolete robot from destruction.

YALSA Science Fiction Genre Committee: Paul Ritz, Clearwater, FL, chair; Mary Arnold, Medina, OH; Candace V. Conklin, Thonotosassa, FL; Phyllis D. Fisher, Brooklyn, NY; Chapple Langemack, Issaquah, WA; Caryl McKellar, Gainesville, FL; Lola H. Twubert, Evansville, IN.

D's Picks

Willis, Connie. *The Doomsday Book.*

Gould, Steven C. *Jumper.*

Kindl, Patrice. *Owl in Love.*

Schmitz, James H. *The Witches of Karres.*

Bujold, Lois McMaster. *Barrayar.*

L'Engle, Madeleine. *A Wrinkle in Time.*

Fantasy

> I read fantasy for the escapism. Fantasy allows me to
> experience things and see things that I would probably
> never have thought of doing or be able to do. Also, because
> it allows me to use my imagination and stay a child just
> that much longer.
>
> —R. Preston Sheldon, age 19

Fantasy is the world of magic, of inexplicable occurrences that don't
have a foundation in reality. It is the realm of Faerie, dragons, unicorns, and
sorcerers. Fantasy is also travel through time and dimensions to alternate
realities that do not necessarily share the same physical laws as our world.
Fantasy does not have to worry if the devices used are logical and possible
in our world as long as they are consistent within the fantasy world.

The near impossibility of really categorizing some titles between fantasy
and science fiction is discussed at the beginning of Chapter 3. In this guide I
am placing novels where I feel they belong. There will, no doubt, be disagree-
ment on the placement of titles and authors between this chapter and the
previous one. The dividing line between horror and fantasy is also fine,
leaving even more room for personal opinion.

SWORD AND SORCERY

Swashbuckling action and daring swordplay in worlds where magic is real
is a brief characterization of this popular and predominant subgenre of fantasy.
For many, sword and sorcery is fantasy. The essence of sword and sorcery is
the conflict between good and evil, combined with magic. The focus may be
on a quest by a party of diverse personalities, or on a heroic figure.

Eddings, David. The Belgariad series: *Pawn of Prophecy, Queen of Sorcery,
Magician's Gambit, Castle of Wizardry,* and *Enchanter's End Game.* The
Mallorean series: *Guardians of the West, King of the Murgos, Demon Lord
of Karanda, Sorceress of Darshiva,* and *The Seeress of Kell.* The Elenium
series: *Diamond Throne, Ruby Knight* and *Sapphire Rose.* The Tamuli
series, *Domes of Fire, The Shining Ones, The Hidden City,* and *Belgarath
the Sorcerer,* with Leigh Eddings.

Feist, Raymond. The Riftwar Saga: *Magician, Silverthorn, Darkness at Sethanon,* and *Prince of the Blood. Magician* was released in two volumes in paperback as *Magician: Apprentice* and *Magician: Master.*

Goodkind, Terry. The Sword of Truth series: *Wizard's First Rule, Stone of Tears,* and *Blood of the Fold.*

Harris, Geraldine. Seven Citadels series: *Prince of the Godborn, The Children of the Wind, The Dead Kingdom,* and *The Seventh Gate.*

Hill, Douglas. *The Blade of the Poisoner. Master of Fiends.*

Jordan, Robert. The Wheel of Time series. *The Eye of the World, The Great Hunt, The Dragon Reborn, The Shadow Rising, The Fires of Heaven, Lord of Chaos,* and *A Crown of Swords.*

Kurtz, Katherine. Chronicles of the Deryni series. Chronicles of Saint Camber series.

McKillip, Patricia A. *The Riddlemaster of Hed.*

Norton, Andre. Witch World series.

Saberhagen, Fred. The Lost Swords series and the Swords series tell the adventures surrounding swords forged in magic and where they were found.

Weis, Margaret, and Tracy Hickman. Darksword trilogy.

Williams, Tad. Memory, Sorrow, and Thorn trilogy: *The Dragonbone Chair, Stone of Farewell,* and *To Green Angel Tower.* Simon, a scullery boy, embarks on a quest to find three swords to save his world from a mad king.

Quest

The quest by an assorted group of companions is one of the most successful subgenres of fantasy. Tolkien's *Lord of the Rings* trilogy has often been imitated and has also inspired a plethora of fantasy novels. Often the quest goes on for several books. Trilogies are common, but if the series sells well they can go into far more volumes. Magic figures prominently.

Brooks, Terry. *The Sword of Shannara. Elfstones of Shannara. Wishsong of Shannara. The Scions of Shannara. Elf Queen of Shannara. The Druid of Shannara. First King of Shannara.*

Brown, Mary. *Pigs Don't Fly.* Somerdai sets out on a quest to find a home and finds she can understand when animals talk to her.

Bujold, Lois McMaster. *The Spirit Ring.* After her sorcerer father is murdered and his spirit enslaved, Fiametta, with the assistance of an earnest young metalworker, sets out to rescue him and free the dukedom.

Douglas, Carole Nelson. The Taliswoman series: *Cup of Clay* and *Seed upon the Wind*. A young woman accidentally stumbles into another world and finds many traveling companions in this first volume of a Tolkien-type series.

Pattou, Edith. *Hero's Song*. In a quest with several stalwart companions, Collum finds his missing sister and learns about his own mysterious past while saving the land from evil invaders.

Silverberg, Robert. *Lord Valentine's Castle*. Valentine and assorted friends journey through Majipoor to regain his throne.

Springer, Nancy. *The Friendship Song*. Two girls travel through a bizarre backyard to arrive in Hades in an attempt to save the life of their favorite rock musician and find the truth of timeless friendship.

Tolkien, J. R. R. *The Hobbit*. *The Lord of the Rings: The Fellowship of the Ring, The Two Towers*, and *The Return of the King*. Possibly the most beloved fantasy ever. Multitudes of sword and sorcery, more specifically quest, fantasies are descendants of "the Trilogy" or its prequel.

Weis, Margaret, and Tracy Hickman. *The Dragonlance Saga*. A motley group of adventurers travel across the land in order to save it from evil.

Heroes and Heroines

People who accomplish larger than life deeds are the protagonists in the following novels. An individual who seems quite ordinary often accomplishes heroic deeds through sacrifice, hard work, and courage.

Alexander, Lloyd. *Westmark. Kestrel. Beggar Queen.*

Cooper, Louise. *The Sleep of Stone*. The last of her race, a shapeshifter tries to marry the mortal that she loves.

Jordan, Sherryl. *Winter of Fire*. Condemned to die on her sixteenth birthday, Elsha is saved by becoming Handmaiden to the Firelord, so that she can free her people.

Jordan, Sherryl. *Wolf-Woman*. Who deserves Tanith's loyalty—the wolves who raised her or the young man she loves?

Lackey, Mercedes. In *The Lark and the Wren*, from the Bardic Voices series, a kitchen drudge travels the world and becomes a bard.

Lee, Tanith. *Black Unicorn*. The daughter of a sorceress, who seems to have no talents other than mechanical, assembles the scattered bones of a unicorn and brings it back to life.

McKinley, Robin. *The Hero and the Crown*. Aerin, a dragon-slaying princess, wins the approval of her father's people. *The Blue Sword* is set in the same land in a different time.

Pierce, Tamora. The Song of the Lioness series: *Alanna: The First Adventure Song of the Lioness, In the Hand of the Goddess, The Woman Who Rides Like a Man,* and *Lioness Rampant.*

Magic

Wizards, sorcerers, mages, witches, and other magic makers are a sub-genre of sword and sorcery where the emphasis is more on the personal growth of the character practicing magic. Rules do apply, so the magic must be consistent in its own milieu.

Ball, Margaret. *Changeweaver. Flameweaver.*

Clayton, Jo. Wild Magic series.

Foster, Alan Dean. Spellsinger series.

Furlong, Monica. *Wise Child. Juniper.*

Hambly, Barbara. The Windrose Chronicles: *The Silent Tower, The Silicon Mage, The Dog Wizard,* and *Stranger at the Wedding.*

Jones, Diana Wynne. *Howl's Moving Castle.*

Zambreno, Mary Frances. *A Plague of Sorcerers. Journeyman Wizard.* A delightful series featuring Jermyn, who with his skunk familiar, Delia, finds himself involved in magical mysteries.

MYTH AND LEGEND

A growing trend in fantasy is to retell the old stories. Robin Hood, King Arthur, and the legends surrounding them are frequent subjects.

Anthony, Piers. Incarnations of Immortality series. *On a Pale Horse,* Thanatos (Death) is personified. *Wielding a Red Sword.* Mars, the god of war, is the protagonist. Other titles in the series deal with fate, earth, good, and evil. *Being a Green Mother. With a Tangled Skein. For the Love of Evil. And Eternity.*

Bradley, Marion Zimmer. *Mists of Avalon.* Lengthy version of the Arthurian legend.

Bradshaw, Gillian. *Hawk of May.* A warrior's version of the Arthurian legend.

Cochran, Molly, and Warren Murphy. *The Forever King.* Arthur Blessing may look like an ordinary child but he holds the Holy Grail by right of birth.

Crompton, Anne Eliot. *Merlin's Harp.* The Arthurian legend told from the viewpoint of Niviene, daughter of the Lady of the Lake.

Dickinson, Peter. *Merlin Dreams*. Dreams of magic visit an enchanted Merlin.

Jones, Courtway. *Witch of the North*. The Arthurian legend from Morgan le Fay's viewpoint. *In the Shadow of the Oak King*.

Lawhead, Stephen R. *Taliesin. Merlin. Arthur*. A Christian retelling of the Arthurian legend.

Llywelyn, Morgan. *Brian Boru: Emperor of the Irish*.

McKinley, Robin. *Outlaws of Sherwood*. A feminist version of Robin Hood.

Rice, Robert. *The Last Pendragon*. A grandson of Arthur tries to make things right.

Roberson, Jennifer. *Lady of the Forest*. A prequel, this story tells of the assemblage of the well-known characters of the Robin Hood legend.

Shwartz, Susan. *The Grail of Hearts*. Based on Wagner's opera *Parsifal*.

Stewart, Mary. *The Hollow Hills, Enchanted Cave. The Wicked Day*. A romantic retelling of Merlin's tale from a master of romantic suspense.

White, T. H. *The Once and Future King*. The classic version of the Arthurian legend starting with *The Sword in the Stone*. *Book of Merlyn* is a sequel.

Woolley, Persia. *Child of the Northern Spring. Queen of the Summer Stars. Guinevere: The Legend in Autumn*. Arthurian trilogy focusing on Guinevere.

Wein, Elizabeth. *The Winter Prince*. Medraut (Mordred) is a healer and the bastard son of King Arthur.

FAIRY TALES

Retelling fairy tales and old folk tales is a growing trend. Some of the stories told in the following novels will be familiar, while others will seem new but have that underlying feeling of having been told before. Tor Books Fairy Tale series created by Terri Windling was written for adults but appeals to mature teens. Talking of the books in this series Lisa Goldstein wrote "difficult truths can sometimes only be told through the medium of fantasy."

Cherryh, C. J. *Rusalka*. In pre-Christian Russia, two fleeing men become involved with Eveshka, a Rusalka, or ghost of a murdered girl, who is trying to return to life.

McKinley, Robin. *Deerskin*. Unveils the horrors of incest in a tale of a beautiful princess and her dog.

Napoli, Donna Jo. *The Magic Circle*. A dark retelling of the Hansel and Gretel fairy tale that changes one's view of the villain and hero.

Thomas, Joyce Carol. *When the Nightingale Sings*. A fairy tale combining gospel music and the story of Cinderella with a African American spin.

Weis, Margaret, and Tracy Hickman. Rose of the Prophet series, based on Middle Eastern tales, complete with djinns.

Wrede, Patricia C. *Snow White and Rose Red*.

Yolen, Jane. *Briar Rose*. Combines the tale of Sleeping Beauty with the horrors of the Holocaust.

Not all fantasy based in fairy and folk tales is dark, some is light and humorous. In fact, many of the stories included in the humorous fantasy section have a foundation in the old stories.

HUMOROUS FANTASY

Frequently humorous fantasy includes elements of familiar fairy and folk tales. Often full of "in jokes," they present more humor to the well-read.

Anthony, Piers. The Xanth series is full of puns and plays on words. *Question Quest*, the fourteenth in the series, recaps many of the earlier events.

Asprin, Robert. The M.Y.T.H. series with humorous titles for the humorous tales. *Hit or MYTH. Little MYTH Marker. MYTHing Link*.

Brooks, Terry. Magic Kingdom of Landover series.

DeChancie, John. Castle Perilous series.

Friesner, Esther. *Majyk by Accident*. A stunned magician's future is changed by a dimension-traveling cat.

Gaiman, Neil, and Terry Pratchett. *Good Omens: The Nice and Accurate Prophecies of Agnes Nutter, Witch*. A demon and an angel try to stop the Apocalypse because they are having too good a time to see it all end.

Jones, Diana Wynne. *Howl's Moving Castle*. When seventeen-year-old Sophie is transformed into a seventy-year-old crone she seeks relief by decamping in a mobile castle belonging to a mysterious wizard. A sequel, *Castle in the Air*, brings Arabian tales into the mix.

Pratchett, Terry. The Book of Nomes series: *Truckers, Diggers,* and *Wings*. A race of tiny beings exists on the edge of our world. A group finds that they must move on when the department store they inhabit is closed.

Turtledove, Harry. *The Case of the Toxic Spell Dump*. Accidents can happen even on magic carpets, and a wild series of events turns an inspector for the Environmental Perfection Agency into a detective.

Watt-Evans, Lawrence, and Esther Friesner. *Split Heirs.* Triplets are split up at birth, the girl to be raised as a prince (yes, prince) and the two princes to be raised as a magician's apprentice and a shepherd.

Wrede, Patricia C. A series featuring tongue-in-cheek humor and an assortment of characters that lurk just on the edge of familiarity. *Dealing with Dragons.* Princess Cimorene searches for happiness and fulfillment by moving in with a dragon. *Searching for Dragons.* The king of the enchanted forest meets a most unusual princess and together they are able to save the kingdom. Others in the series are *Calling on Dragons* and *Talking to Dragons.*

A BESTIARY

Animals, real and imaginary, are found often in fantasy. They display unusual communication skills.

Unicorns

Often portrayed as one-horned horses, unicorns in the following books are viewed in different ways.

Bishop, Michael. *Unicorn Mountain.* The problems of unicorns dying in another dimension and the AIDS epidemic intersect.

Anthony, Piers. *Unicorn Point.*

Beagle, Peter. *The Last Unicorn.*

Brooks, Terry. *The Black Unicorn.* In this volume of the Landover series, a fictional unicorn finds himself brought to life outside his magical book.

Coville, Bruce. Unicorn Chronicles. The first book is *Into the Land of the Unicorns.*

Lee, Tanith. *Black Unicorn.* Untalented in magic, a mechanically minded sorceress' daughter assembles bones to bring a unicorn to life. *The Gold Unicorn* is a sequel.

Salitz, Rhondi Vilott. *The Twilight Gate.* A unicorn, along with forces of evil, cross through a gate fifteen-year-old George creates with his art.

Pierce, Meredith Ann. *Birth of the Firebringer. Dark Moon.* A young unicorn saves his clan by bringing them fire.

Dragons

Dragons are often portrayed as telepathic creatures. There are many different ways of portraying dragons in fiction and this has been so throughout history. Think of the differences between Western and Eastern dragons as portrayed in art and craft.

Bradshaw, Gillian. *The Land of Gold*.

Fletcher, Susan. *Dragon's Milk*.

Fletcher, Susan. *Flight of the Dragon Kyn*. A young woman who was twice spared by dragons is commanded to call them to the waiting archers of the king.

Hambly, Barbara. *Dragonsbane*.

McCaffrey, Anne. The Dragonriders of Pern series: *Dragonflight, Dragonquest*, and *The White Dragon*. Harper Hall trilogy. In these books and others set on the planet of Pern, genetically engineered dragons, mind-linked with humans, teleport and time travel to keep the planet safe.

Murphy, Shirley Rousseau. The Dragonbards trilogy: *Nightpool, The Ivory Lyre*, and *The Dragonbards*. The Dragonbards struggle against armies of the un-men who thrive on human pain.

Norton, Andre, and Mercedes Lackey. *The Elvenbane. Elvenblood.* In a world ruled by evil elves, a halfling human befriends shapeshifting dragons and finds that not all elves are bad.

Rowley, Christopher. *Battle Dragon*.

Strickland, Brad. *Dragon's Plunder*. Jamie Falconer, who has the ability to whistle the wind, is kidnapped and taken aboard a pirate ship that is on a quest to steal a dragon's horde.

Velde, Vivian Vande. *Dragon's Bait*. Left as a sacrifice for a dragon, a young woman instead befriends him, and helps him take revenge on the villagers responsible for her father's death.

Wrede, Patricia C. *Dealing with Dragons. Searching for Dragons. Calling on Dragons. Talking to Dragons.*

Yep, Laurence. Shimmer and Thorn sequence: *Dragon of the Lost Sea, Dragon Steel, Dragon Cauldron,* and *Dragon War.* Genetically engineered dragons.

Yolen, Jane. *Here There Be Dragons*. Stories and poems of dragons. The Pit Dragons trilogy: *Dragon's Blood, Heart's Blood*, and *A Sending of Dragons*.

Uncommon Common Animals

Adams, Richard. *Watership Down*. Rabbits.

Bell, Clare. *Ratha's Creature. Ratha and Thistle-Chaser.* Cats.

Hawdon, Robin. *A Rustle in the Grass*. Ants.

Jacques, Brian. The Redwall series where mice and rats battle evil. *Redwall. Mariel of Redwall. Salamandastron. Martin the Warrior.*

Murphy, Shirley Rousseau. *Nightpool*. Otters.

Williams, Tad. *Tailchaser's Song*. Cats.

Wilson, David Henry. *The Coachman Rat*. Robert may have started out as a human, but he has been transformed into a rat.

Telepathic Animals

A psionic bond between humans and animals is a very popular premise. Anne McCaffrey's dragons and Mercedes Lackey's horse-like companions are telepathic steeds, while Gayle Greeno's ghatti are large cat-like creatures.

Greeno, Gayle. The Ghatti's Tale series: *Finders-Seekers, Mindspeakers' Call*, and *Exiles' Return*.

Lackey, Mercedes. *Arrows of the Queen. Arrow's Flight. Arrow's Fall*.

McCaffrey, Anne. The Harper Hall of Pern trilogy: *Dragonsong, Dragonsinger*, and *Dragondrums*. These books were written for teens and feature fire lizards—tiny relatives of the dragons who figure in McCaffrey's Pern books.

Pierce, Tamora. The Immortals series: *Wild Magic, Wolf-Speaker*, and *Emperor Mage*. Daine empathically communicates with a wolf pack and has the ability to shift into an animal shape.

FAERIE

The world of Faerie is not the same as the world of fairy tales. It is a place of elven people with magical powers. The interaction of humans and residents of Faerie often sets up the conflict. Time moves at a different pace in this world that coexists side by side with ours. Sometimes a rift between the worlds allows someone of Faerie into our world or the reverse. There also seems to be a great proclivity for humans and those of Faerie blood to fall in love. The Faerie folk derived from Celtic folklore are often referred to as Sidhe.

Dean, Pamela. *Tam Lin*. A young woman rescues her love from the Queen of Faerie.

Goldstein, Lisa. *Strange Devices of the Sun and Moon*. An Elizabethan stationer believes that her son may be the changeling prince of Faerie.

Kushner, Ellen. *Thomas the Rhymer*. Thomas's disappearance into the Faerie realm told from varying points of view.

Sherman, Josepha. *Child of Faerie, Child of Earth*. A prince of Faerie and a girl of Earth find love.

Sherman, Josepha. *Windleaf*. A human count goes on a quest to win the hand of a princess of Faerie.

Sherman, Josepha. *Strange and Ancient Name*. A prince of Faerie must sojourn in the world to find out his family history to defeat a curse.

Wrede, Patricia C. *Snow White and Rose Red*. Blanche and Rosamund come to the rescue of the changeling son of the Queen of Faerie.

URBAN FANTASY

The cyberpunk of the fantasy world. Magic and technology share a place in gritty, dangerous cities. Drugs, racism, gangs, and other scourges of modern life are evident.

Brust, Steven, and Megan Lindholm. *The Gypsy*.

Bull, Emma. *War for the Oaks. Finder*. The tale of Orient who gets dragged into a drug dealing scheme that threatens to destroy Bordertown.

Charnas, Suzy McKee. The Sorcery Hill trilogy: *The Bronze King, The Silver Glove,* and *The Golden Thread*. Valentine Marsh fights evils from another universe.

De Lint, Charles. *Dreams Underfoot. Jack of Kinrowan*.

Lackey, Mercedes and others. Serrated Edge series.

Shetterly, Will. *Elsewhere. Nevernever*. The stories of Ron Starbuck who runs away to Bordertown, a place between our world and the Faerie world.

Windling, Terri. *Bordertown*. Tales of Bordertown and its inhabitants.

ALTERNATE
AND PARALLEL WORLDS

Alternate and parallel worlds in fantasy are usually reached by magical or inexplicable means. They are lands where magic is possible. Sometimes the characters who are transported from our world attain fantastic powers.

Anthony, Piers. The Apprentice Adept series: *Split Infinity, Blue Adept, Juxtaposition, Out of Phaze, Robot Adept, Unicorn Point,* and *Phaze Doubt*.

Ball, Margaret. *Lost in Translation*.

Brooks, Terry. The Magic Kingdom of Landover series: *Magic Kingdom for Sale . . . Sold! The Black Unicorn, Wizard at Large, The Tangle Box,* and *Witches' Brew*. In *Magic Kingdom for Sale . . . Sold!* Ben cashes out his life to buy a kingdom in this lighthearted fantasy series.

Dehaven, Tom. *Walker of Worlds*.

Donaldson, Stephen R. The Chronicles of Thomas Covenant series. In two grim trilogies a leper goes into an alternate world.

Duane, Diane. *So You Want to Be a Wizard*. A lighter version of travel to an alternate universe.

Gurney, James. *Dinotopia: A Land Apart from Time*. Lavishly illustrated fictional journal where dinosaurs have an advanced culture.

Jones, Diana Wynne. *A Sudden Wild Magic*. The magicians of Urth inflict their problems on Earth so they can learn how the witches of England would remedy them.

Kay, Guy Gavriel. *The Summer Tree.*

Levy, Robert. *Escape from Exile*. Inexplicably transported to another world, Daniel discovers he can communicate with some rather unusual animals.

Lewis, C. S. The Chronicles of Narnia: *The Lion, the Witch and the Wardrobe, Prince Caspian, The Voyage of the Dawn Treader, The Silver Chair, The Horse and His Boy, The Magician's Nephew,* and *The Last Battle.* While written for, read, and enjoyed by children, this series is still beloved by teens.

O'Donohoe, Nick. *The Magic and the Healing*. A group of veterinary students cross into another world to doctor a unicorn and others.

Weis, Margaret, and Tracy Hickman. The Death Gate Cycle: *Dragon Wing, Elven Star, Fire Sea, Serpent Mage, The Hand of Chaos, Into the Labyrinth,* and *The Seventh Gate.* Four sundered worlds are explored in a series of seven lengthy novels.

TIME TRAVEL

Tales of unexplainable time travel, where a character is just snatched away from his or her own time and deposited in another, provides a rich setting for storytelling, romance, and adventure. Berkley has jumped on the time travel bandwagon with its Anywhere Ring series for younger teens written by Louise Ladd.

Bond, Nancy. *Another Shore*. Working at a historical site in costume precipitates a journey into the past.

Cooney, Caroline B. *Both Sides of Time*. Annie falls in love and through time to 1895.

Gabaldon, Diana. *Outlander. Dragonfly in Amber. Voyager.* A twentieth century nurse/physician travels to eighteenth century Scotland and finds her true love. These extremely lengthy novels were written for adults but are enjoyed by older teens.

Griffin, Peni R. *Switching Well*. Two girls, two eras, and one well that switches them in time.

L'Engle, Madeleine. *An Acceptable Time*. Polly travels 3,000 years into the past to the time of druids.

Lindbergh, Anne. *Nick of Time*. Nick, a boy from 2094, shows up at the Mending Wall school in 1994.

Parks, Ruth. *Playing Beatie Bow*. Abigail finds that she was meant to go back in time.

Tepper, Sheri S. *Beauty*. Beauty travels through time to a future without magic.

Velde, Vivian Vande. *A Well-Timed Enchantment*. A young teen goes back in time when she accidentally drops her watch down a well. Her only friend, a cat, is turned into a boy and carried back to medieval times with her.

Yolen, Jane. *The Devil's Arithmetic*. Hannah is thrust back in time to a Polish village and ends up in a Nazi concentration camp.

PSIONIC ABILITIES

The possession of paranormal powers is an enticing subject. Psionic powers can include telepathy, or the power to communicate mind to mind; teleportation, or the ability for the mind to transport the body from place to place; telekinesis, or the ability to mentally move objects; and precognition, or the ability to see the future. The decision of whether these are SF or fantasy is an extremely difficult one. Stories of psionic powers can be found in both genres.

Greeno, Gayle. The Ghatti's Tale series: *Book One: Finders-Seekers, Mind-speakers' Call*, and *Exiles' Return*. Large telepathic cat-like creatures are bonded with human truth seekers.

Lackey, Mercedes. Heralds of Valdemar, and Mage Winds trilogies. Telepathic links bind heralds and their horse-like companions together.

Springer, Nancy. *The Hex Witch of Seldom*. A girl discovers she has second sight.

FANTASY
ROLE PLAYING GAMES

Fantasy Role-Playing Games (RPG) are really shared world stories created in a game where the players develop personas and experience adventures. TSR, the gaming company, has become a successful publisher distributing novels based on their *Dungeons and Dragons* role-playing games. Fasa Corporation has also had great success with novels based on their Shadowrun game. Many of these fantasy novels verge on horror with vampires, werewolves, and other types of shapeshifters playing important roles. White Wolf has a very successful line of novels based upon their Storyteller System. And over the past year Wizards of the Coast has published several books based on their popular game *Magic the Gathering*. Popular authors writing these novels include:

Christie Golden

Dan Parkinson

Elaine Bergstrom

J. Robert King

James Lowder

Margaret Weis and Tracy Hickman

P. N. Elrod

R. A. Salvatore

Robert Thurston

Nigel Findley

Some names of series that fall into this area are:

Al-Qadim

Dark Sun

Dragonlance

Forgotten Realms

GreyHawk

Ravenloft

Shadowrun

Spelljammer

GRAPHIC NOVELS

Sometimes described as overgrown comics, graphic novels feature stories set to artwork. Usually the violence is also graphic. Not all graphic novels fall into the fantasy and science fiction genres. Art Speigelman's *Maus* and *Maus II* depicts mice in the roles of Jews during the Holocaust. Those works may be the best-known graphic novels in schools and libraries, but if teens are asked they will frequently come up with more. Reviews for graphic novels are hard to come by. Occasionally VOYA reviews a few. VOYA features a column in its pages, written by Kat Kan, that deals with graphic novels and teens. *Publishers Weekly* call this subgenre trade comics rather than graphic novels and generally review titles intended for a much more mature audience. Many graphic novels are restricted for sale to individuals over 18, but even so, many older teens are familiar with and avidly read them.

Fortunately there are now bibliographic guides to these books. *Graphic Novels* by D. Aviva Rothschild (Libraries Unlimited, 1995), a self-proclaimed graphic novel evangelist, provides an enthusiastic look at this area with astute reviews along with important bibliographic information. Steve Weiner's *100*

Graphic Novels for Public Libraries was published in 1996 by Kitchen Sink Press.

Barr, Mike W., and Brian Bolland. *Camelot 3000.* King Arthur is brought into the future.

Gaiman, Neil. Sandman series. A fantasy series with a strong mythological foundation, regarded by many as the best example of graphic novels.

Moore, Alan, and Dave Gibbons. *Watchmen.* The story of superheroes and their fall from grace.

Pini, Wendy and Richard Pini. Elfquest series. A series of high fantasy stories featuring elves and magic that has spawned novels in other subgenres.

Talbot, Bryan. *The Tale of One Bad Rat.* A sexually abused teen is on her own with only a rat for true friendship.

TOPICS

YALSA Fantasy Genre List

The Young Adult Library Services Association of the American Library Association has compiled annotated lists of paperback books. The books "were selected by professional teams of school and public librarians for their popularity as well as literary merit. YALSA has made an effort to include a wide variety of titles to appeal to a range of reading levels, ages, and interests."

Alcock, Vivien. *The Monster Garden.* Dell. $2.95 (ISBN 0-440-40257-3).
Finding a mysterious substance in her genetic engineer father's laboratory, Frankie grows a most unusual "monster."

Alexander, Lloyd. *The Remarkable Journey of Prince Jen.* Dell. $3.99 (ISBN 0-440-40890-3).
Six unusual gifts help a young prince on his adventure quest that pits good against evil.

Anthony, Piers. *Killobyte.* Ace Books. $5.50 (ISBN 0-441-44425-3).
When a teenage computer hacker drives his video dragons too far, a game turns deadly.

Bradley, Marion Zimmer. *Mists of Avalon.* Ballantine. $12.95 (ISBN 0-345-35049-9).
A magical, feminist retelling of the Arthurian legend.

Dexter, Susan. *Wizard's Shadow.* Ballantine. $4.95 (ISBN 0-345-3864-9).
A dead wizard steals Crocken's shadow to avenge his own murder.

Esquivel, Laura. *Like Water for Chocolate.* Anchor Books. $5.99 (ISBN 0-385-42017-X).
A magical story about water, food, cooking, and love. Recently turned into a critically acclaimed movie.

Friesner, Esther. *Majyk by Accident.* Ace Books. $4.99 (ISBN 0-441-51376-X).
When student magician Kendar Gangle acquires the biggest supply of majyk on the planet Orbix, the results are, well, amazing!

Furlong, Monica. *Juniper.* Random House. $3.99 (ISBN 0-679-83369-2).
In this prequel to *Wise Child*, Juniper uses her training in the healing arts to outwit the evil witch Meroot.

Green, Sharon. *Silver Princess, Golden Knight.* Avon. $4.99 (ISBN 0-380-766-25-6).
Strong-willed Alexia matches wits with an arrogant mercenary in this saga of shape shifting, conquest, and surrender.

Hambly, Barbara. *Stranger at the Wedding.* Ballantine. $5.99 (ISBN 0-345-38097-5).
Student wizard Kyra uses unconventional spells to return home and free her sister from impending doom.

Jacques, Brian. *Salamandastron.* Ace Books. $4.99 (ISBN 0-441-00031-2).
The Redwall saga continues as the villainous weasel Ferahgo the Assassin attacks the castle of Salamandastron.

Lee, John. *Unicorn Quest.* Tor Books. $3.99 (ISBN 0-8125-2055-6).
Lady Marianna and young apprentice mage Jarrod search for unicorns, the only hope to save their threatened world.

Mahy, Margaret. *The Changeover: A Supernatural Romance.* Puffin. $3.99 (ISBN 0-14-036599-0).
How can Laura save her little brother whose life force is being drained by the evil Carmody Bracque?

McKinley, Robin. *Deerskin.* Ace Books. $4.99 (ISBN 0-441-00069-X).
Fleeing from her father's unwanted attentions, Lisar struggles to heal herself through the powers of magic and love.

Service, Pamela F. *The Reluctant God.* Fawcett Juniper. $3.99 (ISBN 0-449-70339-8).
A modern-day girl and an ancient Egyptian boy-god meet in a fantastic quest.

Shusterman, Neal. *The Eyes of Kid Midas.* St. Martins. $3.99 (ISBN 0-8125-3460-3).
Magic sunglasses that change wishes to reality begin to take control of Kevin's world in this darkly humorous, fast-paced novel.

Singer, Marilyn. *California Demon.* Hyperion. $3.95 (ISBN 0-78681012-2).
Laura and Danny move from Vermont to Los Angeles, unknowingly accompanied by a wild and crazy imp.

Sleator, William. *Others See Us.* Dutton. $4.99 (ISBN 0-524-45104-8).
After an accident, Jared discovers he can read minds and what he learns about his family is disturbing . . . and dangerous.

Smith, L. J. *Night of the Solstice*. HarperCollins. $3.99 (ISBN 0-06-106172-7). Queen Morgana is captured and children must rescue her with the aid of a wolf in this compelling story of parallel worlds accessed by mirrors.

Wrede, Patricia C. *Talking to Dragons*. Scholastic. $3.99 (ISBN 0-590-48475-3). DayStar is aided by a special sword in his battle to rescue his father, the King of the Enchanted Forest.

YALSA Fantasy Committee Members: Paulette Goodman, Lisle, IL, Chair; Golda B. Jordan, Morgan City, LA; Melanie W. Lightbody, Newport, OR; Cindy Lombardo, Medina, OH; Karen F. Morgan, Denton, TX; Judith Rodriguez, New York, NY.

Short Stories

Galloway, Priscilla. *Truly Grim Tales*. The retelling of fairy tales for teens is not confined to novel length. There are also collections of fairy tales humorously altered for teen tastes.

Kerr, Katharine, ed. *The Shimmering Door*. Stories of sorcerers and shamans, witches and warlocks, enchanters and spell-casters, magicians and mages.

Gaiman, Neil, and Ed Kramer, eds. *Sandman: Book of Dreams*. A shared world anthology set in the world created in Gaiman's graphic novels.

Stearns, Michael, ed. *A Wizard's Dozen*. Thirteen new fantasy stories with unique visions, most by authors already popular with teens.

Bibliographies

Lynn, Ruth N. ed. *Fantasy Literature for Children and Young Adults*, 4th ed. R. R. Bowker, 1995. Annotations of fantasy literature for grades six through twelve.

Online Resources

The Online Resources Section of chapter 3 lists resources for both SF and fantasy.

D's Picks

Brown, Mary. *Pigs Don't Fly*.

McKinley, Robin. *The Hero and the Crown*.

Norton, Andre and Lackey, Mercedes. *The Elvenbane*.

Shetterly, Will. *Nevernever*.

Zambreno, Mary Frances. *A Plague of Sorcerers*.

Mystery, Suspense, and Horror

Horror books terrify the reader and lend enough suspense throughout to capture the reader and create a habit of page turning.

—Kristin Dreves, age 14

Horror is the best—who cares about the rest?

—Cara Mangold, age 12

Teens like to be horrified. They watch horror movies and among their favorite authors are Stephen King, Christopher Pike, and Mary Higgins Clark, all of whom have won book awards voted on by teens. Stephen King has received the Colorado Blue Spruce Award twice, Mary Higgins Clark once, and along with Christopher Pike they have been nominated many times. Many of the authors whose books appear in this chapter write in several subgenres of the suspense, horror, and mystery genres. Determining what falls into each subsection is just as difficult as the division between science fiction and fantasy. One publisher may label a title suspense but the same publisher may label a very similar novel as horror (or sometimes even the same one at a different time). Horror, suspense, and mystery overlap to such an extent that they should be considered together. Readers of one type may very well like another.

MYSTERY

Few mysteries are written for teens compared to the vast number produced for adults. Many of the mysteries written for teens are combined with other genres. The Mystery Writers of America award an annual Edgar Allan Poe Award in the area of Best Young Adult Mystery, but often the nominees seem to be far from traditional mystery. The 1993 winner was *A Little Bit Dead* by Chap Reaver, much more a western than a mystery. *The Weirdo* by Theodore Taylor was also a winner of that award. Mary Frances Zambreno has two mystery titles in her fantasy series dealing with Jermyn, a young wizard in training, and his familiar, Delia, a skunk. The Christian publisher, Bethany House, has introduced the Jennie McGrady Mysteries; titles in the series include *Too Many Secrets, Silent Witness*, and *Pursued*.

Another aspect that allows for a broader range and more titles in adult mystery is that adult detectives can be police, private, or amateur. Teen sleuths, by virtue of their age, must be amateurs.

Many teen readers have recently read the enjoyable mystery adventures found in children's books and consider them too young. The Nancy Drew Files and Hardy Boy Files are, however, written for a slightly older crowd. The Nancy Drew On Campus series is expressly for teens.

Goldman, E. M. *Getting Lincoln's Goat.* Elliot gets some experience in his planned career when he tries to solve the mystery behind the disappearance of Lincoln High School's mascot.

Guy, Rosa. *The Disappearance: A Novel.* Imamu Jones is the prime suspect in the disappearance of Perk, the youngest child of the people who have taken Imamu in.

Haynes, Betsy. *Deadly Deception.* Ashlyn finds more than she bargained for when she attempts to solve the murder of her favorite adult.

Howe, James. *Dew Drop Dead.* A disappearing body involves three teens in an investigation.

Johnston, Norma. The *Delphic Choice.* Meredith's summer visit to Istanbul becomes dangerous when her uncle, a hostage negotiator, disappears.

Kerr, M. E. *Fell. Fell Down. Fell Back.* Fell goes to an exclusive prep school posing as someone else and finds murder and mystery.

McFann, Jane. *One Step Short.* Cath investigates a hit and run death.

Nixon, Joan Lowery. *The Weekend Was Murder. A Dark and Deadly Pool.* Working at a luxury hotel can be more mysterious than expected, especially when bodies turn up.

Nixon, Joan Lowery. *High Trail to Danger. A Deadly Promise.* Set in Leadville, Colorado in 1879. Sarah searches for her missing father then tries to clear his name.

Pullman, Philip. *The Ruby in the Smoke. The Tiger in the Well. The Shadow in the North.* A trilogy of mysteries set in Victorian England with Sally Lockheart, an independent young woman, as the protagonist.

Schwandt, Stephen. *The Last Goodie.* Now that he is in high school he tries to find out what happened to his baby-sitter who disappeared when he was little.

Springer, Nancy. *Toughing It.* One minute Tuff was riding behind his brother on a motorcycle and the next minute Dillon was dead. Tuff needs to find out who killed his brother and why.

Westall, Robert. *A Place to Hide.* Lucy's father has a secret so dangerous that she is sent into hiding with a suitcase of money. She must change her name, her appearance, and her entire life.

Zambreno, Mary Frances. *A Plague of Sorcerers. Journeyman Wizard.* A delightful series featuring Jermyn, who finds himself involved in magical mysteries with his skunk familiar, Delia.

Perhaps one of the reasons so few mysteries seem to be written specifically for teens is because they read adult mysteries. Authors popular with teens are Lillian Jackson Braun, Sue Grafton, Sue Henry, Robert B. Parker, and Tony Hillerman.

SUSPENSE

Suspense books involve a danger from a mortal source even though sometimes the source may seem supernatural. There are many books that seem to be horror with supernatural events, but the denouement proves that the evil was instigated by one all-too-human. The evil in suspense novels come from two major types of deranged individuals—stalkers and psychopaths. Murder is often involved. The authors writing in this subgenre tend to be quite prolific. The books are often labeled as horror novels.

Psychopaths

The psychopath is a deranged person who stalks, takes hostage, or wantonly murders other characters. In teen fiction, the stalker is by far the most common psychopath, but others abound, especially in adult horror novels read by teens. Psychopaths are the villains in most of the best-selling horror novels. In novels written specifically for teens the psychopath is often extremely manipulative even if not murderous.

Most of the following authors write prolifically in this subgenre.

R. L. Stine

Christopher Pike

Joan Lowery Nixon. *Don't Scream.*

Richie Tankersley Cusick

Diane Hoh

Richard Posner

Sharon E. Heisel. *Eyes of a Stranger.*

Some novels of this type that are written for adults but enjoyed by teens are:

Andrews, V. C. *Flowers in the Attic. Petals on the Wind. Seeds of Yesterday. If There Be Thorns. Heaven.* The horror in these modern gothic tales is made more terrible because the psychopaths are family members. V. C. Andrews died in 1987 but left behind synopses of many more books that have been written by others after her death, but published under her name.

Craig, Kit. *Gone*. A couple of teens and a younger sibling go after their kidnapped mother and her abductor.

Strieber, Whitley. *Billy*.

Stalkers

The stalkers in the teen suspense genre are frequently other teens who have become deranged after witnessing a death or being injured. Often, terrifying incidents occur that seem to have no rational explanation until the end. Supernatural events throughout the novel are explained away at the conclusion.

The following list is by no means comprehensive or even extensive. It is only to demonstrate examples of the subgenre.

Baron, Nick, and Michele Nicholas. *Doppelgangers*.

Cusick, Richie Tankersley. *April Fools. Vampire. Silent Stalker. Star Struck.*

Duncan, Lois. *Don't Look Behind You. I Know What You Did Last Summer.*

Koontz, Dean R. *Hideaway*.

McFann, Jane. *Be Mine*.

Miklowitz, Gloria D. *Desperate Pursuit*.

Nixon, Joan Lowery. *The Other Side of Dark*.

Pike, Christopher. *Master of Murder*.

Stine. R. L. *Sunburn*.

HORROR

Horror can be found in many guises. It can be the traditional ghost story, or the gory and graphic splatterpunk. Whatever type it is, though, the purpose is generally to scare the reader.

Paranormal Powers

In stories featuring psionic powers (telepathy, precognition, telekinesis, and teleportation), the dividing line between science fiction, fantasy, and horror is extremely fine.

The novels included here do have horror elements, but could also easily fit into the other genres.

Duncan, Lois. *The Third Eye*.

King, Stephen. *Firestarter*. Drug experiments lead to the birth of a girl who can start fires with her mind.

Pike, Christopher. *Witch*.

Sleator, William. *Others See Us*. After exposure to toxic waste, new mind reading abilities expose the evil in a family.

Smith, L. J. Dark Visions Trilogy: *The Strange Power*, *The Possessed*, and *The Passion*.

Psychological Horror

The manipulation of an individual or group of people is the driving force in this subgenre. As in the suspense novels about stalkers and psychopaths, incidents sometimes seem to have supernatural elements but can usually be attributed to the manipulation by a group of conspirators or a deranged or evil individual by the end. This subgenre overlaps with suspense.

Avi. *Wolfrider*.

Littke, Lael. *Watcher*. Catherine's life starts to parallel that of soap star Cassandra Bly, but then events begin to grow sinister.

Sebestyen, Ouida. *Girl in the Box*. Jackie is inexplicably kidnapped and locked into a damp, lightless room where she starts typing letters to her parents in this truly terrifying tale.

Sleator, William. *House of Stairs*. Teens are the subject of a terrible behavioral experiment. Very frightening.

The Occult and Supernatural

Evil events and evil beings, inexplicable happenings, malevolent forces, and unseen horrors contribute to the scariness of the following stories. Horror featuring the occult and supernatural is one of the favorite genres of teens and the one that is most disapproved of by parents and other adults. The following authors write themes that inspire terror. They write for adults but are very popular with teens.

Blatty, William Peter

Farris, John

Grant, Charles

King, Stephen

Koontz, Dean R.

McCammon, Robert R.

O'Brien, Fitz-James

Poe, Edgar Allan

Straub, Peter

Strieber, Whitley

Several authors write prolifically and specifically for teens in this genre.

Bates, A.

Carmody, Isobelle. *The Gathering*. A terrifying stench permeates a quiet town.

Cooney, Caroline B.

Duncan, Lois. *Stranger with My Face*.

Hoh, Diane

Lake, Simon

Peel, John. *Maniac. Shattered. Talons.*

Pike, Christopher

Sleator, William. *Spirit House*. Exchange student Bia from Thailand seems to have made some kind of pact with a spirit.

Steiner, Barbara

Stine, R. L.

Westwood, Chris. *He Came from the Shadows*.

HORROR SERIES

Horror series are very popular. Even though they are labeled horror, sometimes they are really more mystery and suspense. It is hard to keep a series going when many of the characters are killed off. The way that series can continue in the horror genre is by basing it on a setting rather than on continuing characters. Some series are:

Hodgman, Ann. Children of the Night series.

Hoh, Diane. Nightmare Hall.

Morse, Eric. Friday the Thirteenth: Tales from Camp Crystal Lake.

Pickford, Ted. Scared to Death.

Pine, Nicholas. Terror Academy.

Rue, T. S. Nightmare Inn.

Smith, L. J. Forbidden Game Trilogy: *The Hunter, The Chase*, and *The Kill*. Nightworld series.

Stine, R. L. Fear Street.

Bruce Coville's Chamber of Horrors.

Freddy Krueger's Tales of Terror.

MONSTERS, WEREFOLK, AND OTHER BEASTIES

Whether born or created, these monsters all pose some kind of threat.

Blair, Cynthia. Dark Moon Legacy: *The Curse, The Seduction,* and *The Rebellion.*

Daniels, Zoe. Year of the Cat: *The Dream* and *The Hunt.*

King, Stephen. *Cycle of the Werewolf.*

Koontz, Dean R. *Watchers.* Something evil created in a laboratory is coming closer and closer.

Locke, Joseph. *Kiss of Death.*

Saul, John. *Creature.* A monstrous football team.

Smith, Wayne. *Thor: A Novel.* In this Best Books for Young Adults selection, a German shepherd strives to protect his human pack from the evil of a werewolf in their midst.

Peel, John. *Dances with Werewolves.*

VAMPIRES

The undead, those who suck blood by night, are one of the most popular horror villains or heroes, depending of course, on one's point of view. While all of the following are read by teens, some have adult content.

Carr, A. A. *Eye Killers.*

Hahn, Mary Downing. *Look for Me by Moonlight.*

Hambly, Barbara. *Those Who Hunt the Night.*

Huff, Tanya. *Blood Price. Blood Trail. Blood Pact. Blood Lines.* In this series written for adults but enjoyed by teens, a private investigator and her two boyfriends, one a cop and one a vampire, join forces to combat evil in Toronto.

Klause, Annette Curtis. *The Silver Kiss.* Zoe and Simon become involved in a vampire romance as her mother lays dying. This is the quintessential teen vampire novel.

Locke, Joseph. Blood and Lace Duology: *Vampire Heart* and *Deadly Relations.*

Peel, John. *The Last Drop.*

Pierce, Meredith Ann. Darkangel trilogy: *Darkangel, A Gathering of Gargoyles,* and *The Pearl at the Soul of the World.*

Pike, Christopher. The Last Vampire series.

Rice, Anne. *The Vampire Lestat. Interview with the Vampire. The Queen of the Damned. The Tale of the Body Thief.* (adult)

Saberhagen, Fred. *The Dracula Tapes. The Holmes-Dracula Files. An Old Friend of the Family. Thorn. Dominion. A Matter of Taste. A Question of Time. Seance for a Vampire.*

Smith, L.J. *Secret Vampire. Daughters of Darkness.*

Stine, R. L. *Goodnight Kiss.*

Stoker, Bram. *Dracula.*

Velde, Vivian Vande. *Companions of the Night.*

Yarbro, Chelsea Quinn. *Darker Jewels. Better in the Dark.*

GHOSTS

The stories involving ghosts often involve some poignant aspects of the dead trying to finish business left by an untimely death.

Buffie, Margaret. *Someone Else's Ghost.*

Garfield, Leon. *The Empty Sleeve.*

Henry, Maeve. *A Gift for a Gift: A Ghost Story.*

Hotze, Sollace. *Acquainted with the Night.* Molly and Caleb try to solve the mystery of a ghost that appears to them.

Michaels, Barbara. *Ammie Come Home. A Stitch in Time.*

Nixon, Joan Lowery. *Whispers from the Dead.* After moving into a new house in a new city, Sarah believes something ghostly is trying to contact her about a murder.

Peck, Richard. *Voices after Midnight.* Ghosts from the past have something to say about an antique elevator.

Peck, Richard. *The Ghost Belonged to Me. Ghosts I Have Been.* Blossom Culp, a clever ghost, appears in these humorous tales.

Pike, Christopher. *Remember Me.* Shari Cooper's ghost tries to find out how she died because she is certain she did not commit suicide.

Regan, Dian Curtis. *Jilly's Ghost.* Jilly communicates with the ghost that has been in her backyard all of her life.

Reiss, Kathryn. *Time Windows.* Miranda is haunted by ghostly experiences she has when looking into an antique replica of her home.

Siegel, Barbara, and Scott Siegel. *Final Frenzy.*

Sweeney, Joyce. *Shadow.* The ghost of Sarah's beloved cat tries to lead her out of danger.

WITCHES

Gilmore, Kate. *Enter Three Witches*. Bren's life is complicated by the presence of too many witches. A humorous and romantic tale.

Mahy, Margaret. *The Changeover: A Supernatural Romance.*

Smith, L. J. *Spellbinder*. Two teenage witches fall for the same human boy.

UNEXPLAINED PHENOMENA

Duncan, Lois. *Locked in Time*. Is it possible that Nore's new stepmother is really over 100 years old?

Westall, Robert. *Yaxley's Cat*. Everyone is afraid of the family who has moved into Yaxley's abandoned home.

Whittington, Don. *Spook House*. Brock Poe visits a relative who owns the ancestral home, The House of Usher.

MEDICAL HORROR

It is terrifying when something goes terribly wrong in the arena that is supposed to provide healing. Evil people preying on patients, stealing organs, or performing diabolical experiments, are major themes in medical horror written by Robin Cook and others.

Cook, Robin. *Coma. Mutation. Fatal Cure. Blindsight.*

Dickinson, Peter. *Eva*. After surviving a horrible wreck, Eva discovers that her brain has been transplanted into the body of a chimpanzee.

Shelly, Mary. *Frankenstein*. The original story of medical horror written when the author was in her teens.

Stevenson, Robert Louis. *Dr. Jekyll and Mr. Hyde*. When a medical experiment goes awry, Henry finds out that you cannot destroy evil.

Splatterpunk

Graphic horror, with lots of blood and guts and other disgusting props, delight some teens. Slasher movies like the *Friday the 13th* and *Nightmare on Elm Street* series are the film parallel to splatterpunk novels. Often teens will go to the adult section of a library for books by Clive Barker, Joe Lansdale, Poppy Z. Brite, David Schow, and others. No one is writing or publishing splatterpunk specifically for the teen market.

TOPICS

Bibliographies

Many of the sources for science fiction also include horror.

Online Resources

HWA, the Horror Writers Association, maintains a home page at http://www.greyware.org/hwa. Information on horror books and authors can also be found at many of the science fiction sites.

Anthologies

The short story is an excellent medium for horror. Many are published each year, often with an emphasis on a subgenre.

Coville, Bruce. *Chamber of Horrors. Oddly Enough.*

Greenberg, Martin H., ed. *Werewolves.*

Jones, Stephen, ed. *The Mammoth Book of Werewolves.*

Pike, Christopher. Tales of Terror Anthology series.

Preiss, Byron, ed. *The Ultimate Werewolf.*

Yolen, Jane. *The Faery Flag: Stories and Poems of Fantasy and the Super-natural.* Eerie and funny stories of the supernatural.

Yolen, Jane, and Martin H. Greenberg, eds. *Vampires.* An anthology of shorter vampire tales.

YALSA Genre Lists

MYSTERY GENRE LIST

Every young adult loves to solve a puzzle or figure out a complex riddle—and that's exactly what reading a good mystery is like. The books chosen for this list all have solvable crimes and logical clues that allow the reader to unravel the mystery. Plots twist and turn, characters appear and disappear. Reading mysteries is an excellent activity for young adults. It helps build critical thinking skills, and it can foster a genuine appreciation for leisure reading that will last a lifetime.

Mote. Reaver, Chap. Dell. 0-440-21173-5. 1992. Paper $3.50. Mote, a Vietnam vet and loner, is suspected of murdering one of Chris's high school teachers.

Who Killed My Daughter? Duncan, Lois. Dell. 0-440-21342-8. 1994. Paper $5.99. In a bizarre parallel to her novels, Duncan's own daughter is murdered and her family must go into hiding.

The Weirdo. Taylor, Theodore. Avon Flare. 0-380-72017-5. 1993. Paper $3.50. Samantha Sanders, 16, befriends Chip Clewt, the "Weirdo" who lives in the Powhatan Swamp, scene of two violent murders.

Whispers from the Dead. Nixon, Joan Lowery. Dell 0-440-20809-2. 1991. Paper $3.50. As Sarah unravels a murder mystery, a stalker plans her death.

Murder on the Iditarod Trail. Henry, Sue. Avon. 0-380-71758-1. 1993. Paper $4.99. Someone is murdering the mushers!

The Client. Grisham, John. Dell 0-440-21352-5. 1994. Paper $6.99. Witnessing a Mafia suicide has Mark running from both the bad guys and the good guys.

Ghost Abbey. Westall, Robert. Scholastic. 0-590-41693-6. 1990. Paper $2.95. Moving into an ancient abbey proves dangerous for Maggi and her family.

Incident at Loring Groves. Levitin, Sonia. Fawcett. 0-449-70347-9. 1990. Paper $2.95. Teens find a dead body in the park but choose to remain silent.

Bum Steer. Pickard, Nancy. Pocket Books. 0-671-68042-0. 1991. Paper $4.99. Jenny Cain dons cowboy boots to investigate a foundation grant and discovers mystery in the death of a multimillionaire rancher.

Hound of the Baskervilles. Doyle, Sir Arthur Conan. New American Library. 0-451-52478-0. 1986. Paper $3.40. Sherlock Holmes must decide if the death of Sir Charles Baskerville is due to a family curse or murder most foul.

The Tiger in the Well. Pullman, Philip. Borzoi Sprinters. 0-679-82671-8. 1992. Paper $4.50. Sally Lockhart has never met Arthur Parrish, but he has proof they are married! A sinister and swift-moving Victorian mystery.

Fell Down. Kerr, M. E. Harper Trophy. 0-06-447086-5. 1993. Paper $3.95. Seventeen-year-old Fell's investigation into his best friend's death leads him to a ventriloquist's convention.

The Trouble with Lemons. Hayes, Daniel. Fawcett Juniper. 0-449-70416-5. 11992. Paper $3.99. Self-styled "lemons," Tyler and Lymie find a dead body floating in the local quarry.

A Is for Alibi. Grafton, Sue. Bantam. 0-553-27991-2. 1987. Paper $5.99. California P. I. Kinsey Milhone's first case involves an eight-year-old murder.

Someone's Mother Is Missing. Mazer, Harry. Dell. 0-440-21097-6. 1991. Paper $3.50. When Lisa's mother disappears, she and Cousin Sam reluctantly team up to launch a search before it's too late.

Stonewords: A Ghost Story. Conrad, Pam. Harper Trophy. 0-06-440354-8. 1991. Paper $3.95. A girl and her ghost companion solve an age-old mystery.

Coyote Waits. Hillerman, Tony. Harper Paperbacks. 0-06-109932-5. 1992. Paper $5.99. Officer Jim Chee of the Tribal Police arrests Navaho Ashie Pinto for the murder of Chee's friend, Nez.

Silver Pigs. Davis, Lindsey. Ballantine. 0-345-36909-6. 1991. Paper $4.99. Ancient Roman sleuth Marcus Didius Falco is hired to discover who is stealing the Emperor's silver.

Blood Shot. Paretsky, Sara. Dell. 0-440-20420-8. 1989. Paper $5.99. V. I. attends a reunion of her high school basketball team and winds up courting murder.

All That Remains. Cornwell, Patricia D. Avon. 0-380-71833-2. 1993. Paper $5.99. Dr. Kay Scarpetta is baffled by a series of ritualistic "couple killings."

YALSA Mystery Genre Committee: Suzanne Manczuk, Plainsboro, NJ, Chair; Lynn Crockett, Nutley, NJ; Barbara Hardt, Crystal Lake, IL; Janice Hogan, Topeka, KS; R. J. Pasco, Lincoln, NE; Carol Truett, Boone, NC; Laura Weber, Los Angeles, CA.

HORROR GENRE LIST

In this age of high technology, young adults continue to be intrigued by the unknown. They love to be frightened, and good horror stories can and do frighten, as they suspend the reader's and the character's safety. Horror may contain elements of the supernatural, pits good against evil with the opportunity for evil to win, and offers an emotional intensity with a promise of violence that is usually fulfilled. Horror manipulates reality, haunting the reader even after the last page has been turned.

Mother's Helper. Bates, Autine. Scholastic. 0-590-44582-0. 1991. Paper $3.25. Becky is going to need all the help she can get.

The Beast. Benchley, Peter. Fawcett. 0-449-22089-3. 1992. Paper $5.99. "It hovered in the ink-dark water, waiting."

Stranger. Cooney, Caroline B. Scholastic. 0-590-45680-6. 1993. Paper $3.50. Nicoletta is obsessed by Jethro, who lives beyond the dead end.

Gone. Craig, Kit. Berkley. 0-425-13944-1. 1994. Paper $5.50. While Michael and his baby brother are looking for their lost mother, someone is looking for them.

Teacher's Pet. Cusick, Richie Tankersley. Scholastic. 0-590-43114-5. 1990. Paper $3.25. Kate's vacation at a summer writing camp is a real lesson in horror.

The Stalker. Davidson, Nicole. Avon 0-380-76645-0. 1992. Paper $3.50. Who is stalking whom in the mall?

Camp Fear. Ellis, Carol. Scholastic. 0-590-46411-6. Who is terrorizing the counselors at Camp Silverlake?

The Fever. Hoh, Diane. Scholastic. 0-590-45401-3. 1992. Paper $3.25. Twelvetrees Community Hospital is no place to be sick.

Four Past Midnight. King, Stephen. New American Library Dutton. 0-451-17038-5. 1991. Paper $6.99. Four stories from another dimension.

Game Over. Locke, Joseph. Bantam. 0-553-29652-3. 1993. Paper $3.40. Here's a video arcade where you play like the devil. . . .

Nightwaves: Scary Tales for After Dark. McDonald, Collin. HarperTrophy. 0-06-440447-1. 1992. Paper $3.95. Eight stories about ghosts, curses, and magic.

Urban Horrors. Nolan, William, ed. DAW. 0-88677-548-5. 1993. Paper $5.50. Mean streets and lonely alleys are "terror-ibble."

The Witching Hour. Rice, Anne. Ballantine. 0-345-38446-6.1993. Paper $6.99. The Mayfair family legacy of witchcraft is alive and well.

Summer of Night. Simmons, Dan. Warner Books. 0-446-36266-2. 1992. Paper $5.99. Teens battle against the evil face that has taken over their school.

Secret Circle: The Initiation, vol. 1. Smith, L. J. Harper. 0-06-106712-1. 1992. Paper $3.99. The Salem legend lives on.

Curtains. Stine, R. L. Pocket Books. 0-671-69498-7. 1990. Paper $3.50. Will the last act end in murder?

Ghost Stories. Westall, Robert, comp. Kingfisher. 1-85697-884-2. 1993. Paper $6.95. Twenty-two tales of the supernatural by masters of the form.

He Came from the Shadows. Westwood, Chris. Fawcett. 0-449-70430-0. 1992. Paper $3.99. Dreams can come true—for a price. . . .

The Christmas Killer. Windsor, Patricia. Scholastic. 0-590-43310-5. 1992. Paper $3.25. Rose's gift is the only thing that can stop the killer.

Vampires. Yolen, Jane and Martin H. Greenberg, eds. HarperTrophy. 0-06-440485-4. 1993. Paper $3.95. Where you least expect them.

YALSA Horror Genre List Committee: Jack Forman, San Diego, CA, Chair; Jan Chandra, Greensboro, NC; Deborah D. Taylor, Baltimore, MD; Ellen C. Thompson, Westminster, CO; Anne Sheehan, Wellesley, MA.

D's Picks

Pike, Christopher. *Remember Me.*

Pullman, Philip. *The Ruby in the Smoke.*

Sleator, William. *Others See Us.*

Smith, Wayne. *Thor: A Novel.*

Velde, Vivian Vande. *Companions of the Night.*

Adventure

The thrill of beating the odds and surviving adversity is part of the attraction of adventure. The characters are often easy to identify with, having many traits in common with teens. Adventure is a popular theme in young adult literature appearing in several genres. Fantasy, science fiction, mystery, suspense, and horror all have strong elements of adventure.

SURVIVAL

A particular appeal of survival stories is the teen protagonist testing the limits, possibly making life-threatening mistakes, but triumphing over adversity in the end. The threats to survival can be physical or psychological. The danger may come from the environment, the situation, or the other characters in the story.

Bell, William. *Forbidden City*. Canadian Alex finds himself in the midst of the Tiananmen Square massacre of 1989.

Bunting, Eve. *Jumping the Nail*. Sometimes survival means defying peer pressure.

Campbell, Eric. *Place of Lions*. A fourteen-year-old saves the lives of his father and the pilot after a plane crash in the Serengeti.

Carter, Alden R. *Between a Rock and a Hard Place*. Cousins on a Minnesota canoe trip face a deadly peril after their food is eaten by a bear.

Cole, Brock. *The Goats*. Survival on the run after being selected to face humiliation by their fellow summer campers.

Cooney, Caroline B. *Flash Fire*. A group of teens fight against a raging fire in a canyon near Los Angeles.

Cottonwood, Joe. *Danny Ain't*. Danny hides the fact that he is on his own when his father is hospitalized for post-traumatic stress.

Cottonwood, Joe. *Quake!* The lives of Franny and others are changed when the big earthquake hits.

Defoe, Daniel. *Robinson Crusoe.* The classic tale of survival on a desert island.

George, Jean Craighead. *Julie of the Wolves.* Julie, a Native-American girl, befriends a wolf pack after becoming lost in the Alaskan wilderness.

Hobbs, Will. *Beardance.* In this sequel to *Bearstone*, Cloyd, a young Ute, lives with two grizzly cubs high in the San Juans as winter approaches.

Hobbs, Will. *Downriver.* A group of teens take their own trip on the unpredictable waters of the Colorado river.

Hobbs, Will. *The Big Wanderer.* A fourteen-year-old spends the summer on his own in the Southwest looking for his uncle.

Holman, Felice. *Slake's Limbo.* Urban survival in the underground world of the subway system.

Kelleher, Victor. *Rescue! An African Adventure.* When Dave and Jess try to stop the experimentation on two baboons, they become the hunted.

Miklowitz, Gloria D. *After the Bomb.* Philip Singer finds himself in charge of his family after a nuclear bomb explodes.

Morey, Walt. *Death Walk.* After stowing away on a small plane, Joel finds himself alone in the Alaskan wilderness on the run from the killers who torched the plane.

Morpurgo, Michael. *Waiting for Anya.* Jo and others in a small French village help Benjamin smuggle Jewish children across the border to Spain.

Nance, John J. *Pandora's Clock.* This adult book, popular with teens, tells of an airplane denied the right to land because a passenger is suspected to have an Ebola-like virus.

Paulsen, Gary. *Hatchet.* A hatchet makes the difference between life and death for the lone survivor of a plane crash in a remote part of Canada. *The River.* Brian once again faces survival challenges after he goes into the wilderness and his companion ends up in a coma.

Paulsen, Gary. *The Voyage of the Frog.* Survival at sea.

Paulsen, Gary. *The Haymeadow.* John is alone in the high country keeping watch over a huge flock of sheep with only four dogs and two horses for companionship.

Roper, Robert. *In Caverns of Blue Ice.* Mountaineering.

Ruckman, Ivy. *No Way Out.* A group of hikers is stranded in a narrow canyon by a flash flood.

Sweeney, Joyce. *Free Fall*. Four boys are trapped in a cave.

Taylor, Theodore. *The Cay*. A young American and an old black sailor are marooned on a tiny cay. *Timothy of the Cay*. The prequel/sequel, telling how Timothy ended up where he did and what happened after the events in *The Cay*.

White, Robb. *Deathwatch*. Ben must survive being hunted down in the desert.

Whittaker, Dorothy Raymond. *Angels of the Swamp*. One fleeing the prospect of foster care and the other an alcoholic father, two teens make a life for themselves in the swamps of Depression-era Florida.

WAR

Novels of war combine survival and loss with adventure.

Dickinson, Peter. *AK*. Fictional African revolution and coup.

Garfield, Brian. *The Paladin*. World War II.

Marsden, John. *Tomorrow, When the War Began*. A group of Australian teens return home from a camping trip to find their country has been invaded.

Mazer, Harry. *The Last Mission*. World War II.

Myers, Walter Dean. *Fallen Angels*. Vietnam.

Noonan, Michael. *McKenzie's Boots*.

Reuter, Bjarne. *The Boys from St. Petri*. World War II.

Rylant, Cynthia. *I Had Seen Castles*. World War II.

Westall, Robert. *Blitzcat*. World War II, starring a cat!

Willard, Nancy. *Things Invisible to See*. World War II.

EXPLORATION

Arkin, Anthony Dana. *Captain Hawaii*. On vacation in Hawaii, Arron is drawn into a madcap adventure in an untamed area.

Bosse, Malcolm. *Deep Dreams of the Rain Forest*. In Borneo of World War II, fifteen-year-old Harry joins the quest of two young headhunters.

Ferris, Jean. *All That Glitters*. Dreading a summer to be spent with his distant father, the hero finds a job scuba diving to help find a lost Spanish galleon.

Marino, Jose Maria. *Dreams of Gold*. The son of a conquistador joins an expedition of exploration.

Paulsen, Gary. *Canyons*. A century after Coyote Runs was killed by U.S. soldiers, Brennan Cole, a fourteen-year-old on a camping trip, finds his skull. Both young men's coming-of-age stories are interwoven.

Rostkowski, Margaret I. *Moon Dance*. A group of teens goes on a backpacking trip to check out observations made in a diary by a pioneer woman in Utah's canyon country.

Strasser, Todd. *Beyond the Reef*. A search for undersea treasure.

Ullman, James Ramsey. *Banner in the Sky*. Rudi is compelled to conquer the mountain that killed his father.

TECHNOTHRILLER/ESPIONAGE

Emerging in the 1980s in adult fiction, technothrillers are just now appearing for teens. Many science fiction novels for teens feature strong techno elements. Tom Clancy's technothrillers are popular with teen readers as are those of Stephen Coonts. Espionage novels for teens usually feature a teen whose parents are involved in espionage activities.

French, Michael. *Split Image*.

French, Michael. *Circle of Revenge*.

Ottley, Ted. *Code of Deception. Code of Roadies*.

HEROISM

Putting one's life or happiness on the line to help others is what heroism is all about. The following books feature individuals who don't set out to be heroic but end up that way.

Cooney, Caroline B. *Flight Number 116 Is Down*. When a plane crashes on her family's estate, a young woman, along with several other teens, finds out what heroism is.

Mikaelsen, Ben. *Sparrow Hawk Red*. In a far-fetched but fun tale, Ricky Diaz steals an airplane to get even with the drug cartel that killed his mother.

Philbrick, Rodman. *Freak the Mighty: A Novel*. Max and Freak, two outcasts, are great together, especially after Max is kidnapped by Killer Kane.

Reuter, Bjarne. *The Boys from St. Petri*. Several young men gradually find themselves sabotaging the Nazis.

Shusterman, Neal. *Speeding Bullet*. Nick Herrera inadvertently becomes a celebrity after he heroically saves a child.

TOPICS

Adventure is one area that is shockingly short on bibliographies. It was not a genre chosen by YALSA for the genre lists even though it is a popular genre with teens. Many of the books found in this chapter did appear on other genre lists indicating the overlap and blending of genres.

D's Picks

Carter, Alden R. *Between a Rock and a Hard Place.*

Cole, Brock. *The Goats.*

Hobbs, Will. *Beardance.*

Myers, Walter Dean. *Fallen Angels.*

Philbrick, Rodman. *Freak the Mighty: A Novel.*

Contemporary

I like to read sports fiction because it shows the struggles
that athletes encounter and also expands my knowledge
about the specific sport.
—Kristin Dreves, age 14

The here and now is easy to relate to even when situations are not. The contemporary teen novel can take many different forms, from the most psychologically daunting problem novel, to the bildungsroman, to the hilarious comedy. The topics can range from first love and sibling rivalry to the deadly serious topics of incest, AIDS, and abuse.

Contemporary teen romance will be found in the romance chapter. Some titles will appear in both chapters.

COMING OF AGE

One of the biggest challenges we face as human beings is going from the status of child, dependent on parents or guardians, to the status of being adults, responsible for our own lives. The bildungsroman, or coming-of-age novel, most often involves the teen years, the important time when the transition from childhood to adulthood is traveled. The coming-of-age novel is appealing in that it often provides characters and events easy for teen readers to identify with. One of the most famous coming-of-age novels, *Catcher in the Rye* by J. D. Salinger, is still read by teens. Some of the following novels deal with seeking self-identity as the protagonist grows to adulthood, while some deal with the search for identity faced by an adopted teen. Some coming-of-age novels feature serious and thoughtful growth while the other end of the spectrum combines humor with the process of proceeding beyond childhood.

Avi. *Blue Heron*.

Bauer, Joan. *Squashed*.

Berg, Elizabeth. *Durable Goods*.

Brooks, Martha. *Two Moons in August.*
Carter, Alden R. *Dogwolf.*
Cole, Brock. *Celine.*
Cooney, Caroline B. *Flight Number 116 Is Down.*
Crutcher, Chris. *Ironman.*
Davis, Jenny. *Checking on the Moon.*
Davis, Terry. *If Rock and Roll Were a Machine.*
Deaver, Julie Reece. *Chicago Blues.*
Hall, Barbara. *Fool's Hill.*
Hall, Lynn. *Flying Changes.*
Johnson, Angela. *Toning the Sweep.*
Grant, Cynthia D. *Keep Laughing.*
Guy, Rosa. *The Music of Summer.*
Keegan, John E. *Clearwater Summer.*
Lasky, Kathryn. *Memoirs of a Book Bat.*
MacDonald, Caroline. *Speaking to Miranda.*
MacLachlan, Patricia. *Journey.*
Merrick, Monte. *Shelter: A Novel.*
McKenna, Colleen O'Shaughnessy. *The Brightest Light.*
Moore, Martha. *Under the Mermaid Angel.*
Mori, Kyoko. *One Bird. Shizuko's Daughter.*
Myers, Walter Dean. *Somewhere in the Darkness.*
Okimoto, Jean Davies. *Molly by Any Other Name.*
Peck, Richard. *Princess Ashley.*
Peck, Sylvia. *Kelsey's Raven.*
Pfeffer, Susan Beth. *Most Precious Blood.*
Plummer, Louise. *My Name Is Sus5an Smith. The 5 Is Silent.*
Rapp, Adam. *Missing the Piano.*
Rodowsky, Colby. *Hannah in Between.*
Salisbury, Graham. *Blue Skin of the Sea.*
Seabrooke, Brenda. *Bridges of Summer.*
Shoup, Colby. *Wish You Were Here.*
Sweeney, Joyce. *The Tiger Orchard.*
Willey, Margaret. *The Melinda Zone.*
Williams-Garcia, Rita. *Like Sisters on the Homefront.*
Woodson, Jacqueline. *From the Notebooks of Melanin Sun.*

PROBLEM NOVELS

All teens have problems. Sometimes it seems that all teen novels are "problem novels" simply because if teen characters are present, problems are present. The degree of the problems place certain novels here. This section deals with some of the worst things that can happen in the life of a teen.

Death and Deadly Disease

Lurlene McDaniel is the queen of teen death novels. She has even written a series called *One Last Wish* dealing with terminally ill teens. The following novels deal with the effects of death or terminal illnesses of friends and family members on the teen protagonists.

Arrick, Fran. *Where'd You Get the Gun, Billy?* David and Liz are stunned when classmate David shoots his girlfriend Lisa.

Carter, Alden R. *Sheila's Dying.* It's impossible to break up with a girl-friend who is terminally ill.

Coman, Carolyn. *Tell Me Everything.* Roz's mother is killed saving a boy's life.

Deaver, Julie Reece. *You Bet Your Life.* Bess goes to work on a comedy show while recovering from her mother's suicide.

Draper, Sharon M. *Tears of a Tiger.* Driving drunk, Andy killed his best friend in a car accident.

Ferris, Jean. *Signs of Life.* It is hard to love again after sixteen-year-old Hannah loses her twin to death.

Ferris, Jean. *Invincible Summer.* Robin, who has leukemia, finds love with fellow cancer patient Rick.

Grant, Cynthia D. *Shadow Man.* Multiple viewpoints illuminate Gabe's short life. He could have done much had he not wrapped his truck around a tree.

Hesse, Karen. *Phoenix Rising.* Nyle does not even want to know Ezra, who is dying from radiation.

Hosie-Bounar, Jane. *Life Belts.* Nita cares for her dying mother.

Hurwin, Davida Wills. *Time for Dancing.* Two dancers, best friends, must deal with dying when one becomes seriously ill.

Mazer, Harry. *When the Phone Rang.* A family tries to stay together after the parents have died.

Mazer, Norma Fox, and Harry Mazer. *Heartbeat.* Hillary loves both Tod and Amos but a fatal disease comes into this story of broken hearts.

McDaniel, Lurlene. *A Season for Good-bye. She Died Too Young. Baby Alicia Is Dying. Somewhere Between Life & Death.*

Naughton, Jim. *My Brother Stealing Second*. Like his brother Billy, who was killed in a drunk driving accident, Bobby also likes baseball and drinking.

Pershall, Mary K. *You Take the High Road*. Samantha is devastated by the drowning death of her baby brother.

Pullman, Philip. *The White Mercedes*. A young man's prior actions cause the death of the girl he loves.

Shusterman, Neal. *What Daddy Did*. Preston is not only trying to rebuild his life after his mother is killed, but he must also face the fact that his father is the killer.

Strasser, Todd. *Friends till the End*. David befriends Howie, the new kid, who is stricken with leukemia.

Talbert, Marc. *Dead Birds Singing*.

Suicide and Self Destruction

Depression, drug addiction, mental illnesses, and suicide are realities in our society. The following novels can tell the truth of these tragedies more eloquently than nonfiction dealing with the same topics.

Anonymous. *Go Ask Alice*. This anonymous diary of a teen druggie who does not survive is listed by some sources as fiction and by other sources as nonfiction.

Bennett, James. *I Can Hear the Mourning Dove*. Grace Braun, who suffers from depression, attempts suicide after her father's death.

Block, Francesca Lia. *The Hanged Man*. With her father dying in a hospital, Laurel enters into a sexual and drug-using relationship with an older man.

Cadnum, Michael. *Breaking the Fall*. Stan joins his friend Jared in a deadly game of breaking into occupied homes.

Childress, Alice. *A Hero Ain't Nothin' but a Sandwich*. Thirteen-year-old Benjie is a drug addict.

Dale, Mitzi. *Round the Bend*. A teenage girl has multiple personalities.

Dragonwagon, Crescent. *The Year It Rained*.

Ferry, Charles. *Binge*. Eighteen-year-old Weldon, while on a drunken quest for old friends, kills several teens.

Guest, Judith. *Ordinary People*. Conrad has come home from a mental institution after attempting suicide after his brother's accidental death.

LeMieux, A. C. *The T.V. Guidance Counselor*. Seventeen-year-old Michael, in a mental hospital after a leap off a bridge, relates the event that took him there.

Landis, James David. *The Band Never Dances.* Judy finds success as a drummer in a rock band after her older brother commits suicide.

Nixon, Joan Lowery. *Secret Silent Screams.* Barry is dead and everyone believes it was suicide, but Marti is convinced he was murdered.

Peck, Richard. *Remembering the Good Times.* For some people loving friends are just not enough.

Pevsner, Stella. *How Could You Do It, Diane?* Bethany seeks the reason why her beloved stepsister would take a drug overdose.

Pfeffer, Susan Beth. *Family of Strangers.*

Stoehr, Shelley. *Crosses.* Cutting herself is just one of the ways that Nancy tries to ease the pain in her life.

Stoehr, Shelley. *Weird on the Outside.* Sixteen-year-old Tracey runs away to New York City, where she becomes topless dancer Amanda.

Mental Illness

The books in this section, even while having humorous titles, deal with the serious and disturbing issue of teens having to face mental illness in a parent, sibling, or even themselves.

Cannon, A. E. *Amazing Gracie.*

Caseley, Judith. *My Father the Nutcase.*

Carter, Alden R. *RoboDad.* Retitled *Dancing on Dark Water.*

Faustino, Lisa R. *Ash: A Novel.*

Johnson, Angela. *Humming Whispers.*

Naylor, Phyllis Reynolds. *The Keeper.*

Stowe, Rebecca. *Not the End of the World.* Maggie has six personalities.

Sexual Identity

First love and coming of age for a gay boy, a bisexual teen, or lesbian girl presents some problems different than those faced by heterosexual teens. The following books deal with individuals, heterosexual, bisexual, and gay, discovering their own sexual preferences and identities. The pain and issues surrounding coming to terms and coming out as well as the joy of first love and the confusing nature of crushes are found in the following as well. There is an excellent short story anthology, *Am I Blue?* edited by Marion Dane Bauer dealing with the same issues.

Block, Francesca Lia. *Baby Be-Bop.*

Chambers, Aidan. *Dance on My Grave. The Toll Bridge.*

Garden, Nancy. *Annie on My Mind.*

Kerr, M. E. *Deliver Us from Evie.*

Murrow, Liza Ketchum. *Twelve Days in August.*

Walker, Kate. *Peter.*

Weiler, Diana. *Bad Boy.*

Pregnancy and Teen Parents

Even with the escalating rate of teen pregnancy and the prevalence of teens keeping their babies, teens still want to read about how others cope with the situations caused by early parenthood. While most titles feature girl protagonists, Reynolds's *Too Soon for Jeff* and Klein's *No More Saturday Nights* see the situation from the young father's point of view.

Christiansen, C. B. *I See the Moon.*

Cole, Sheila. *What Kind of Love? The Diary of a Pregnant Teenager.*

Doherty, Berlie. *Dear Nobody.*

Farish, Terry. *Shelter for a Seabird.*

Ferris, Jean. *Looking for Home.*

Head, Ann. *Mr. and Mrs. Bo Jo Jones.*

Kaye, Geraldine. *Someone Else's Baby.*

Klein, Norma. *No More Saturday Nights.*

Lettes, Billie. *Where the Heart Is.*

Reynolds, Marilyn. *Detour for Emmy. Too Soon for Jeff.*

Rodowsky, Colby. *Lucy Peale.*

Williams-Garcia, Rita. *Like Sisters on the Homefront.*

Wurmfeld, Faith. *Baby Blues.*

Incest

The conflict that propels the following novels is possibly the most heinous crime visited on some teens.

Block, Francesca Lia. *The Hanged Man.* Laurel takes drugs, starves herself, and has unprotected sex with a mysterious man as she comes to realize that her dead father had sexually abused her.

Crutcher, Chris. *Chinese Handcuffs.* Dillon witnessed his brother's suicide and now he is in love with the sexually abused Jennifer.

Grant, Cynthia D. *Uncle Vampire.* One twin comes to the conclusion that her uncle is a vampire because the truth is too hard to bear.

Hermes, Patricia. *A Solitary Secret.*

Irwin, Hadley. *Abby, My Love.* Abby keeps Chip at a distance because of sexual abuse by her father.

Savage, Georgia. *House Tibet.* Vicky and her autistic brother run away after she is raped by their father.

Voigt, Cynthia. *When She Hollers.* Tish takes a knife and her own life in hand to stop the abuse from her stepfather.

White, Ruth. *Weeping Willow.* A strong girl works to extricate herself from a life with a molesting stepfather.

Woodson, Jacqueline. *I Hadn't Meant to Tell You This.* A middle class African American girl befriends a lonely, abused "white trash" student new to her school.

Physical Challenges

The general American view of teens as carefree, healthy, and strong is not always accurate. There are teens with physical disabilities, caused by genetics defects, disease, or accident. Coming to terms with these conditions at the same time as coming of age is a popular theme.

Bowler, Tim. *Midget.* A fifteen-year-old boy with multiple handicaps is secretly tortured by a cruel older brother.

Brancato, Robin F. *Winning.* Gary is recuperating from the football injury that has paralyzed him.

Calvert, Patricia. *Picking Up the Pieces.* Coming to terms with life after a disabling motorcycle accident.

Covington, Dennis. *Lizard.* Lucius's deformities had kept him in a home for retarded boys even though he was smart.

Crutcher, Chris. *The Crazy Horse Electric Game.* Willy faces the disintegration of his family and homelessness after his brilliant sports potential is crushed in an accident.

Flanigan, Sara. *Alice.*

Forman, Carol. *Chelsey and the Green-Haired Kid.* From her wheelchair under the stands at a basketball game, Chelsey witnesses a murder.

Feuer, Elizabeth. *Paper Doll.* Leslie lost both her legs in a car accident, but that doesn't stop her from playing the violin.

Greenberg, Joanne. *Of Such Small Differences.* A blind, deaf man and an actress fall in love.

Hodge, Lois L. *A Season of Change.* Biney's hearing loss is something she learns she can live with.

Klein, Norma. *My Life as a Body.* Can a paraplegic have sex?

Kerr, M. E. *Little Little.* Little Little Le Belle is a dwarf, but will that stop her from finding love?

McDaniel, Lurlene. *I'll Be Seeing You.* A gorgeous boy blinded in a chemistry experiment and an empathic girl with a facial deformity find love. But will it last if his vision returns?

Philbrick, Rodman. *Freak the Mighty: A Novel.* Max is huge, lonely, and nearly illiterate while brilliant Kevin is tiny and unable even to walk due to birth defects. Kevin on Max's shoulders equals Freak the Mighty, a powerful friendship.

Scott, Virginia M. *Belonging.* Gustie must adjust after meningitis leaves her deaf.

Sirof, Harriet. *Because She's My Friend.* Teri, a hospital volunteer, becomes friends with paralyzed Valerie.

Voigt, Cynthia. *Izzy, Willy-Nilly.* A ride home with a boy who had a few too many costs Izzy her leg.

Politics

The following novels deal with contemporary political situations and issues that affect the teen characters either directly or through effects on their families or communities. These novels provide a connection point for teens who are interested in the global community.

Becerra de Jenkins, Lyll. *Celebrating the Hero.* Camilla, in San Javier for a ceremony to honor her grandfather, finds that forgiveness goes a long way in a family that was not as heroic as she thought.

Buss, Fran Leeper. *Journey of the Sparrows.* Food and jobs are scarce for Maria as she avoids immigration and tries to make a life in the United States.

Covington, Dennis. *Lasso the Moon.* April's life is changed when she meets Fernando, a refugee from the political terror in El Salvador.

Dickinson, Peter. *Shadow of a Hero.* Alternating chapters, interspersed with mythical legends of ancient heroes, tell of a contemporary family's life when the eastern European country they had emigrated from strives for independence after the fall of the Soviet Union.

Laird, Elizabeth. *Kiss the Dust.* Tara and her middle class Kurdish family must flee their home in Iraq.

Slaughter, Charles H. *The Dirty War.* People disappear in Argentina's Dirty War.

Staples, Suzanne Fischer. *Shabanu: Daughter of the Wind*. A nomadic girl is given to an older man to be his fourth wife in contemporary Pakistan. *Haveli*. Shabanu, now the teen mother of a little girl, must be ever vigilant to protect them both in treacherous times.

Temple, Frances. *Grab Hands and Run*. When their father disappears, Felipe, his mother, and sister must escape to the north. *Taste of Salt: A Story of Modern Haiti*.

Thorton, Lawrence. *Naming the Spirits*. A young woman is haunted by ghosts killed in Argentina's Dirty War.

Williams, Michael. *Crocodile Burning*. A South African youth joins the cast of a performing troupe.

Personal Convictions

Teens who take a stand for what they believe in can face conflict and suffer severe consequences for sticking by their guns.

Avi. *Nothing But the Truth*. Philip is suspended from school for humming the national anthem.

Peck, Richard. *The Last Safe Place on Earth*. Censorship.

Ruby, Lois. *Miriam's Well*. The right to refuse medical treatments.

Missing Teen Syndrome

A recent and popular trend has been for a subgenre dealing with the idea of missing children, the ones who are often pictured on milk cartons or on television. Sometimes because of teen-parent conflicts teens wonder if their parents are really theirs, or if they were adopted. Often these novels include strong elements of suspense and mystery.

Bunting, Eve. *Sharing Susan*. After another family's teen daughter dies, Susan is confronted with the fact that she had been switched at birth and is not her parent's child.

Cooney, Caroline B. *The Face on the Milk Carton*. When fifteen-year-old Janie Johnson recognizes her picture as a 3-year-old on a milk carton, she starts a quest for her real identity. In the sequel, *Whatever Happened to Janie?*, she is reunited with the family that has spent years hoping and praying for her return. The two books were recently made into a television movie.

Haynes, Betsy. *Deadly Deception*. Ashlyn is devastated when her beloved school counselor is murdered, but the bequest left to her makes her question her own identity.

Mazer, Harry. *Who Is Eddie Leonard?* After the death of his grandmother, Eddie sees the picture of a missing child and comes to believe that he is the long missing Jason Diaz.

Mazer, Norma Fox. *Taking Terri Muller*. Terri finds the mother whom her father has told her was dead.

Pfeffer, Susan Beth. *Twice Taken*. Brooke sees her dad on a call-in television show about parental kidnapping and changes her whole life by dialing 11 digits.

Pfeffer, Susan Beth. *The Year Without Michael*. The pain and despair that hits a family when a teenage son disappears.

Roybal, Laura. *Billy*. After being arrested in a bar brawl, Billy is discovered to be a kidnapped child who then has to leave his rural mountain life, his truck, family, friends, and girl to go to Des Moines as Will.

Homelessness and Foster Living Arrangements

Teens become homeless for several reasons. Some have run away from untenable home situations, some have run from schools, institutions, or foster care situations. Some of the books in this section are about teens who are homeless because their families are homeless. The feeling of home is an important one, and many of the characters in the following attempt to create a sense of home by forming relationships with others.

Banks, Russell. *Rule of Bone*.

Bennett, James. *Dakota Dream*.

Blacker, Terence. *Homebird*.

Corcoran, Barbara. *Stay Tuned*.

Crutcher, Chris. *The Crazy Horse Electric Game*.

Fox, Paula. *Monkey Island*.

Grant, Cynthia D. *Mary Wolf*.

Hermes, Patricia. *Mama, Let's Dance*.

Holman, Felice. *Slake's Limbo*.

Nasaw, Jonathan Lewis. *Shakedown Street*.

Nelson, Theresa. *Beggar's Ride*

Savage, Georgia. *House Tibet*.

Thesman, Jean. *When the Road Ends*.

Voigt, Cynthia. *Homecoming*.

AIDS

AIDS is affecting more teens every year. There are a few books about teens who contract AIDS and several about a loved one who does.

Arrick, Fran. *What You Don't Know Can Kill You.* The lives of many are changed after a casual encounter at a frat party brings AIDS into the lives of two sisters and their town.

Bess, Clayton. *The Mayday Rampage.* Even the best informed can make mistakes with deadly consequences in this story of a pair of high school journalists.

Durant, Penny Raife. *When Heroes Die.* Gary's adored Uncle Rob is dying of AIDS.

Humphreys, Martha. *Until Whatever.* Popular Karen fights to keep her lab partner Connie from being expelled from school just because she has AIDS.

Kaye, Marilyn. *Real Heroes.* Kevin's father leads the fight to oust Kevin's HIV positive teacher from his teaching job.

Kerr, M. E. *Night Kites.* Erick finds out that his beloved older brother has AIDS and is gay.

Miklowitz, Gloria D. *Good-Bye Tomorrow.*

Nelson, Theresa. *Earthshine.* Slim and Isaiah become friends at a support group for people with AIDS. Her gay father and his pregnant mother are both victims of the disease.

Assault

The following novels deal with the aftermath of violence or rape on both the victims and perpetrators.

Corman, Avery. *Prized Possessions.* Elizabeth precipitates a campus protest when she reports the rape she suffered her first week of college.

Cormier, Robert. *We All Fall Down.* A girl is flung down the stairs when drunken teens trash a house.

Johnson, Scott. *One of the Boys.* Trying to belong, Eric participates in criminal pranks.

Mazer, Norma Fox. *Out of Control.* An unplanned attack on a girl leaves her feeling violated and the three boys in trouble.

Miklowitz, Gloria. *Past Forgiving.* Alexandra is abused by her boyfriend, Cliff.

Peck, Richard. *Are You in the House Alone?* Who would believe that a rich, popular student could be a rapist?

Tamar, Erika. *Fair Game.* A graphic depiction of an incident called a gang rape told from several viewpoints including those of the mentally challenged victim and a boy who didn't do anything to stop it.

Gangs

Forshay-Lunsford, Cyn. *Walk Through Cold Fire.*

Garland, Sherry. *Shadow of the Dragon.* Tragedy strikes Danny's life when a Vietnamese gang and a skinhead gang come into his life.

Hinton, S. E. *The Outsiders. That Was Then, This Is Now.* Gang life in Oklahoma. *The Outsiders* was written while Ms. Hinton was in her teens.

Levoy, Myron. *A Shadow Like a Leopard.*

Mowry, Jess. *Way Past Cool. Six Out Seven.* Contemporary, realistically depicted gang life.

Myers, Walter Dean. *Scorpions.* Jamal is told by his jailed brother to take over leadership of his gang, the Scorpions.

Crime and Criminals

Cadnum, Michael. *Taking It.* Anna, a chronic shoplifter, worries about her grip on sanity.

Cooney, Caroline B. *Driver's Ed.* Stealing traffic signs seems like a harmless prank until Remy learns of the deadly consequences.

Marsden, John. *Letters from the Inside.* Two girls exchange letters and lies.

Obsfeld, Raymond. *The Joker and the Thief.* Griffin is an escapee from a juvenile correctional facility.

Ruby, Lois. *Skin Deep.* Relocating and having a hard time fitting in, Dan joins up with a neo-Nazi skinhead group.

HUMOROUS NOVELS

Not all contemporary issues are dealt with in a heavy or intense way. Humor is a delightful stress reliever and also illuminates some of the everyday weirdness that makes life so interesting. While laugh out loud funny, the humor in some of the following is a counterpoint to serious teen issues.

Arter, Jim. *Gruel and Unusual Punishment.*

Bauer, Joan. *Squashed. Thwonk.*

Block, Francesca L. *Weetzie Bat.*

Clarke, J. *The Heroic Life of Al Capsella. Al Capsella and the Watchdogs. Al Capsella Takes a Vacation.*

Conford, Ellen. *Genie with the Light Blue Hair*. If there is any way for a wish to go awry it will. *Dear Lovey Hart: I Am Desperate*.

Deaver, Julie Reece. *You Bet Your Life*.

Danziger, Paula. *The Cat Ate My Gymsuit. The Pistachio Prescription. Divorce Express. There's a Bat in Bunk Five*.

Fine, Anne. *Flour Babies*.

Hall, Lynn. *Murder in a Pig's Eye*.

Hentoff, Nat. *Does This School Have Capital Punishment?*

James, Mary. *Frankenlouse*. A military academy is not a place for a sensitive cartoonist, but since his family runs the place he doesn't have much choice. *Shoebag*. A cockroach faces the ultimate horror— he is turned into a human! Mary James is a pseudonym of M. E. Kerr.

Karl, Herb. *Toom County Mud Race*.

Kerr, M. E. *Little Little*.

Korman, Gordon. *Don't Care High. Losing Joe's Place. Son of Interflux*.

Koertge, Ron. *Harmony Arms. Arizona Kid. Where the Kissing Never Stops*.

Levitin, Sonia. *The Mark of Conte*.

Lipsyte, Robert. *One Fat Summer*.

Manes, Stephen. *Obnoxious Jerks. Comedy High*.

Marino, Jan. *Like Some Kind of Hero*.

Mazer, Harry. *I Love You, Stupid!*

McCants, William D. *Much Ado About Prom Night*.

McFann, Jane. *Free the Conroy Seven*.

Murphy, Barbara Beasley, and Judie Wolkoff. *Ace Hits the Big Time. Ace Hits Rock Bottom*.

Myers, Walter Dean. *The Mouse Rap. Fast Sam, Cool Clyde and Stuff*.

Pascal, Francine. *My First Love and Other Disasters*.

Peck, Richard. *Those Summer Girls I Never Met*.

Paulsen, Gary. *The Boy Who Owned the School*.

Pinkwater, Daniel. *The Snarkout Boys and the Avocado of Death*.

Pinkwater, Jill. *Buffalo Brenda*.

Shusterman, Neal. *The Eyes of Kid Midas*.

Spinelli, Jerry. *Who Put That Hair in My Toothbrush?*

Stine, R. L. *How I Broke Up with Ernie. Phone Calls*.

Stone, Bruce. *Half Nelson, Full Nelson.*

Vail, Rachel. *Do Over.*

Wersba, Barbara. *The Farewell Kid. You'll Never Guess the End.*

Winton, Tim. *Lockie Leonard, Human Torpedo.*

Wyss, Thelma Hatch. *Here at the Scenic-Vu Motel.*

Zindel, Paul. *The Undertaker's Gone Bananas. Pardon Me, You're Stepping on My Eyeball.*

SPORTS

Often sports novels provide a larger context for exploring other themes, often pithy problems such as incest, loss of a loved one, or child abuse. Many teens participate in sports of one sort or another or participated when younger. The sports setting provides a context to which the reader can relate.

Thomas Dygard, a prolific writer of sports novels, authors books that feature the sports more intensely than most other teen sports novels. He has written on several different sports. Additional straightforward sports stories that concentrate on the sport more than on superimposed problems can be found in sports series books, such as The Rookies.

Baseball

Crutcher, Chris. *The Crazy Horse Electric Game.*

Deuker, Carl. *Heart of a Champion.*

Dygard, Thomas J. *Infield Hit. The Rookie Arrives.*

Freeman, Mark. Rookies paperback series.

Naughton, Jim. *My Brother Stealing Second.*

Powell, Randy. *Dean Duffy.*

Tunis, John R. *Rookie of the Year.*

Weaver, Will. *Striking Out. Farm Team.*

Basketball

Bennett, James. *Squared Circle.*

Brooks, Bruce. *The Moves Make the Man.*

Crutcher, Chris. *Chinese Handcuffs.*

Deuker, Carl. *On the Devil's Court.*

Myers, Walter Dean. *Hoops.*

Boxing

Lipsyte, Robert. *The Contender. The Brave. The Chief.*
Lynch, Chris. *Shadow Brother.*

Football

Baczewski, Paul C. *Just for Kicks*. Humorous.
Crutcher, Chris. *Running Loose.*
Dygard, Thomas J. *Forward Pass.*
Miklowitz, Gloria D. *Anything to Win.*

Hockey

Weiler, Diana. *Bad Boy.*
Lynch, Chris. *Iceman.*

Soccer

Cottonwood, Joe. *Adventures of Boone Barnaby.*
Murrow, Liza Ketchum. *Twelve Days in August.*

Swimming

Crutcher, Chris. *Stotan. Staying Fat for Sarah Byrnes.*
Duder, Tessa. *In Lane Three, Alex Archer.*

Triathlon

Crutcher, Chris. *Ironman.*

Track

Cannon, A. E. *The Shadow Brothers.*
Crutcher, Chris. *Chinese Handcuffs.*
Hoffius, Stephen. *Winners and Losers.*
Hughes, Dean. *The End of the Race.*
Voigt, Cynthia. *The Runner.*

Wrestling

Davis, Terry. *Vision Quest.*
Klass, David. *Wrestling with Honor.*
Spinelli, Jerry. *There's a Girl in My Hammerlock*. Humorous.

TOPICS

YALSA Genre Lists

HUMOR GENRE LIST

Angell, Judie. *Leave the Cooking to Me*. Bantam 0-553-29055-X, $3.50. Fifteen-year-old Shirley makes a bundle while trying to keep her catering business a secret from her mother.

Bauer, Joan. *Squashed*. Dell 0-440-21912-4, $3.99. Growing the largest pumpkin in Iowa turns out to be easier for sixteen-year-old Ellie than losing 20 pounds.

Conford, Ellen. *A Royal Pain*. Scholastic 0-590-43821-2, $2.95. Abby learns she is really Princess Florinda XIV of Saxony Coburn. Long live the—uh, Princess!

Cooney, Caroline B. *Twenty Pageants Later*. Bantam 0-553-29672-8, $3.99. Scottie-Anne finds herself trapped in a beauty pageant.

Fine, Anne. *Alias Madame Doubtfire*. Bantam 0-553-56615-6, $3.99. You saw the movie, now read the book about how Mr. Hilliard becomes Madame Doubtfire to spend more time with his kids.

Hall, Lynn. *Murder in a Pig's Eye*. Harcourt Brace 0-15-256269-9, $4.95. Bodie is convinced Henry Siler killed his wife and buried her on their farm. But where's the body?

Hayes, Daniel. *Eye of the Beholder*. Avon 0-380-72285-2, $3.99. Tyler and Lymie's "discovery" rocks the art world.

Koertge, Ron. *The Boy in the Moon*. Avon 0-380-71474-4, $3.99. Nick learns that he is more than the sum of his pimples. Much more.

Korman, Gordon. *A Semester in the Life of a Garbage Bag*. Scholastic 0-590-44429-8, $3.25. Grandpa is passed off as a dead poet to help Ray and Sean win a trip to Greece.

McCants, William D. *Anything Can Happen in High School: And It Usually Does*. Harcourt Brace 0-15-276605-7, $3.95. The popular kids try to drown the Radical Wave. Everybody out of the pool!

McFann, Jane. *Free the Conroy Seven*. Avon 0-380-76401-6, $3.50. The Conroy Seven are guilty until proven innocent. Confessions, anyone?

Myers, Walter Dean. *The Righteous Revenge of Artemis Bonner*. Harper-Collins 0-06-440462-5, $4.95. Artemis Bonner travels to the Old West to avenge the murder of his Uncle, Ugly Ned. Hilarious complications abound.

Pinkwater, Jill. *Buffalo Brenda*. Atheneum 0-689-71586-2, $3.95. Adopting a bison to serve as their school mascot is the ultimate scheme for wacky compatriots Brenda Tuna and India Ink Teidlebaum.

Powell, Randy. *Is Kissing a Girl Who Smokes Like Licking an Ashtray?* Farrar, Straus & Giroux 0-374-43627-4, $3.95. Biff might be able to answer this if he would kiss Heidi instead of spending all of his time dreaming about Tommie.

Service, Pamela F. *Weirdos of the Universe, Unite!* Fawcett 0-449-70429-7, $3.99. Mythological beings help Mandy and Owen save Earth.

Spinelli, Jerry. *There's a Girl in My Hammerlock.* Simon & Schuster 0-671-86695-8, $3.95. Did Marie join the boy's wrestling team for herself or to win Eric?

Stine, R. L. *How I Broke Up with Ernie.* Paperback Books 0-671-69496-0, $3.50. Horrormeister Stine writes a funny story about a boy named Ernie who doesn't take the hint when Amy breaks up with him.

Wardlaw, Lee. *Seventh Grade Weirdo.* Scholastic 0-590-44806-4, $3.25. Does having a Winnie-the-Pooh family make you weird? Ask twelve-year-old Christopher (Rob) Robin!

Wilson, Johnniece M. *Poor Girl, Rich Girl.* Scholastic 0-590-44733-5, $3.25. Contact lenses = money = a job for unskilled Miranda.

Zable, Rona. *Landing on Marvin Gardens.* Bantam 0-553-29288-9, $3.50. Living with neat busybody Aunt Rose seems like a death sentence to sloppy Kate.

YALSA Humor Genre Committee: Mary Huebscher, Parma, OH, Chair; Janet Ake, Carrollton, TX; Marianne S. Ramirez, Old Tappan, NJ; Norma P. St. Amand, Bloomfield Hills, MI; Cheryl K. Ward, Windsor Locks, CT.

Sports Genre List

Barre, Shelley. *Chive.* Simon & Schuster. $14.00 (ISBN 0-671-75641-9). Quick moves and fast action highlight the skateboard competition.

Bauer, Marion Dane. *Face to Face.* Dell. $3.99 (ISBN 0-440-40791-5). Will a whitewater rafting trip give Michael the chance he needs to prove his courage?

Campbell, Eric. *Shark Callers.* Harcourt Brace. $4.95 (ISBN 0-15-200010-0). A South Seas sailing trip turns deadly as teens face a tidal wave and killer sharks.

Crutcher, Chris. *Staying Fat for Sarah Byrnes.* Delacorte. $3.99 (ISBN 0-4440-21906-X). Can misfits stay friends when "Moby" wins a spot on the swim team?

DeFelice, Cynthia. *Devil's Bridge.* Avon. $3.50 (ISBN 0-380-72117-1). Ben's determination to win the fishing competition almost costs him his life.

Deuker, Carl. *Heart of a Champion.* Avon Flare. $3.50 (ISBN 0-380-72269-0). Baseball brings Seth and Jimmy together; risky behavior drives them apart.

Drumtra, Stacy. *Face Off.* Avon Flare. $3.50 (ISBN 0-380-76863-1). Twin brothers vie to outdo each other on the ice.

Dygard, Thomas J. *Backfield Package.* Puffin. $3.99 (ISBN 0-14-036348-3). Can a football friendship survive the pressures of senior year?

Gutman, Bill. *Shaquille O'Neal.* Pocket Books. $3.50 (ISBN 0-671-88088-8). The story behind the hoopla about the man who fits the size 20 shoe.

Hall, Lynn. *Flying Changes.* Harcourt Brace. $4.95 (ISBN 0-15-228791-4). Romance and rodeos—can they mix?

Henry, Sue. *Murder on the Iditarod Trail.* Avon. $4.99 (ISBN 0-380-71758-1). A killer stalks the leaders of this grueling dog sled race.

Hoffius, Stephen. *Winners and Losers.* Simon & Schuster. $15.00 (ISBN 0-671-79194-X). The state track championship is up for grabs when Daryl's heart stops during a meet!

King, Tabitha. *One on One.* NAL-Dutton. $5.99 (ISBN 0-451-17981-1). A love of basketball draws Deenie the Mutant and Sam together in an unlikely romance.

Lipsyte, Robert. *The Brave.* HarperTrophy. $3.95 (ISBN 0-06-447079-2). Sonny Bear flees the reservation and learns about more than boxing in dangerous New York City.

Lynch, Chris. *Shadow Boxer.* HarperTrophy. $3.95 (ISBN 0-06-447112-8). Two brothers struggle with their father's boxing legacy.

McManus, Patrick. *The Night the Bear Ate Goombaw.* Owl Books. $6.95 (ISBN 0-8050-1340-7). Hiking, fishing, and camping—put 'em together and what've you got? Comedy chaos!

Naughton, Jim. *My Brother Stealing Second.* Trophy Keypoint. $3.95 (ISBN 0-06-447017-2). Bobby is haunted by the accident that killed his older brother, Billy, Ryder High's hope for the major leagues.

Ripslinger, Jon. *Triangle.* Harcourt Brace. $3.95 (ISBN 0-15-200049-6). Joy's chance to lead her softball team to the state tournament is threatened by a secret affair.

Soto, Gary. *Taking Sides.* Harcourt Brace. $6.95 (ISBN 0-15-284077-X). Basketball player Lincoln Mendoza's loyalties are divided when he moves from the inner city to the suburbs.

Wilson, Mike. *Right on the Edge of Crazy.* Random. $11.00 (ISBN 0-679-74987-X). Downhill and dangerous with the U.S. ski team.

Alternates in Priority Order

Rivers, Glenn, and Bruce Brooks. *Those Who Love the Game.* Harper Trophy. $4.95 (ISBN 0-06-446174-2).
Glenn "Doc" Rivers talks compellingly about life in the NBA.

French, Michael. *Pursuit.* Dell. $2.95 (ISBN 0-440-96665-5).
A backpacking trip turns into a life and death struggle.

Puckett, Kirby. *I Love This Game! My Life in Baseball.* Harper. $5.99 (ISBN 0-06-109210-X).
A popular ballplayer's rags to riches story.

Gilbert, Sarah. *A League of Their Own.* Warner Books. $4.99 (ISBN 0-446-36383-9).
Compelling story of the women's professional baseball league, both on and off the diamond.

Hughes, Dean. *One Man Team.* Bullseye Books. $3.99 (ISBN 0-679-85441-X).
Aaron's a basketball hotshot but has he got what it takes to be a team player?

Barkley, Charles, and Roy S. Johnson. *Outrageous!* Avon. $4.99 (ISBN 0-380-72101-5).
Sir Charles, on and off the court. Outrageous!

Anderson, Peggy King. *Safe at Home!* Macmillan. $3.95 (ISBN 0-689-718330-0).
Tony's a star pitcher on the mound but a shameful secret at home leaves less and less time for baseball.

YALSA Sports Genre Committee: Mary Arnold, Medina, OH, Chair; Ellen Alig Duffy, Harlan, IN; Barbara Kubinski, Washington, DC; Melanie P. Myers, Columbus, OH; Elizabeth K. Shuping, Florence, SC.

Short Stories

Gallo, Donald, ed. *Short Circuits.* A humorous horror anthology.

Crutcher, Chris. *Athletic Shorts.*

D's Picks

Crutcher, Chris. *Ironman.*

Grant, Cynthia D. *Shadow Man.*

Lasky, Kathryn. *Memoirs of a Bookbat.*

Roybal, Laura. *Billy.*

Nelson, Theresa. *Earthshine.*

Romance

Romance is one of the largest genres in teen paperback fiction. The Sweet Valley High series has sold millions of copies and spawned gazillions of imitators. Romance plays a major role in the life of most teens, even teens who are not involved in romantic relationships wonder if they should be or wish they were. One way that teen fiction is ahead of adult fiction is that several male authors write of romance from a male point of view. Boys as well as girls experience the agony and ecstasy of young love.

SOAP OPERA

The soap opera subgenre deals with the conflicts and interactions of teen life. The Sweet Valley High series is the type most frequently thought of as teen romance. It has been the prototype for many similar series. The spin-off for younger readers is the Sweet Valley Twins series. Now that that Jessica and Elizabeth have been in high school for several years, those that want to go on can, to the Sweet Valley University series.

Soap opera deals with an ensemble cast, creating the opportunity for endless variations on what can happen in the lives of teens.

Applegate, Katherine. Boyfriends/Girlfriends series.

Applegate, Katherine. Ocean City series.

Baer, Judy. Cedar River Daydreams series. Christian.

Baer, Judy. Live from Brentwood High series. Christian.

Beverly Hills 90210 series. From the popular Fox Network television series.

Class Secrets series.

DeGrassi Junior High series. Based on the Canadian television series.

Distress: Call 911 series.

18 Pine Street series. African American teens.

Love Stories series.

Roommates series.

Summer series. Summer finds a new boyfriend every month.

Sweet Dreams series.

Sweet Valley High series. The "big" one.

Sweet Valley University series. Also known as SVU.

Wild Hearts series. The adventures of an all-girl Nashville rock band.

CONTEMPORARY CHRISTIAN ROMANCE

Romances published by the Christian publishing houses are often as popular with teens as with adults. Reviews have traditionally been sparse. One of the best places to see what is new is on supermarket racks, where Christian publishers have marketed quite successfully. Ingram publishes an edition of *Christian Advance* that identifies the books they stock that fall into the Christian or inspirational areas. *Bookstore Journal* also reviews Christian titles.

Baer, Judy. *A Special Kind of Love.*

Hardy, Robin. *Streiker's Bride. Streiker the Killdeer.*

Rue, Nancy. *The Janis Project.*

Now there are even Christian romance soap opera series written for teens. Bethany House has two; Live from Brentwood High and Cedar River Daydreams, both by Judy Baer. Lauraine Snelling's Golden Filly series has been called a cross between Nancy Drew and Sweet Valley High. Other Christian contemporary series with romance are the China Tate series by Lissa Halls Johnson and the Christie Miller series by Robin Jones Gunn.

CONTEMPORARY ROMANCE

Contemporary romance often involves issues of dysfunctional families, suicidal tendencies, or other pithy social issues, but they do not feature the ensemble cast with the diversity of problems found in soap opera.

Anderson, Mary. *Unsinkable Molly Malone.*

Baker, Carin Greenberg. *A Time to Love. Good-Bye to Love.*

Bell, Mary S. *Sonata for Mind and Heart.*

Blume, Judy. *Forever.*

Caseley, Judith. *Kisses.*

Clements, Bruce. *Tom Loves Anna Loves Tom.*

Davis, Jenny. *Sex Education.*

Hahn, Mary Downing. *The Wind Blows Backwards.*

Hamilton, Virginia. *A White Romance.*

Kaplow, Robert. *Alessandra in Between.*

Kerr, M. E. *Gentlehands.*

LeMieux, A. C. *Do Angels Sing the Blues?*

Levoy, Myron. *Kelly 'n' Me.*

Myers, Walter Dean. *Motown and Didi.*

Qualey, Marsha. *Revolutions of the Heart.*

Tamar, Erika. *The Things I Did Last Summer.*

Wittinger, Ellen. *Lombardo's Law.*

ROMANCE SHORT STORIES

Sometimes a short story is just the right format for telling a tale of romance. The following collections contain some stories that are strong on romance and on contemporary relationships in general.

Brooks, Martha. *Paradise Cafe and Other Stories.*

Mazer, Norma Fox. *Dear Bill, Remember Me.*

HUMOROUS ROMANCE

Romantic comedy often involves relationships that never get off the ground. Some include paranormal events or characters such as genies, witches, or angels.

Bauer, Joan. *Squashed.*

Conford, Ellen. *Loving Someone Else.*

Cooney, Caroline B. *The Girl Who Invented Romance.*

Danziger, Paula. *Remember Me to Harold Square. Thames Doesn't Rhyme with James.*

DeClements, Barthe. *How Do You Lose Those Ninth Grade Blues?*

Gilmore, Kate. *Enter Three Witches.*

Hall, Lynn. *Dagmar Schultz and the Angel Edna. Dagmar Schultz and the Powers of Darkness.*

Hite, Sid. *Answer My Prayer.*

Kaplow, Robert. *Alessandra in Love.*

Kerr, M. E. *Him She Loves?*

Koertge, Ron. *The Boy in the Moon.*

Lewis, Linda. *2 Young 2 Go 4 Boys.*

McFann, Jane. *No Time for Rabbits. Be Mine.*

Neenan, Colin. *In Your Dreams.*

Okimoto, Jean Davies. *Jason's Women.*

Powell, Randy. *Is Kissing a Girl Who Smokes Like Licking an Ashtray?*

Sharmat, Marjorie. *How to Meet a Gorgeous Guy. How to Meet a Gorgeous Girl. He Noticed I'm Alive—And Other Hopeful Signs. Two Guys Noticed Me—And Other Miracles.*

Stine, R. L. *How I Broke Up with Ernie. Phone Calls.*

Thompson, Julian. *Philo Fortune's Awesome Journey to His Comfort Zone.*

Winton, Tim. *Lockie Leonard, Human Torpedo.*

PARANORMAL ROMANCE

Using paranormal or supernatural characters is a growing trend in adult romance that is now moving into teen romance too. The characters can be angels, werewolves, vampires, or even cupids. Sometimes the paranormal characters are a love interest, other times they are there to facilitate romance between mortals.

Bauer, Joan. *Thwonk.* Cupid.

Chandler, Elizabeth. *Kissed by an Angel. The Power of Love. Soulmates.* Angels.

Leroe, Ellen. *Meet Your Match, Cupid Delaney.* Cupid.

Hodgman, Ann. *Dark Music.* Werewolves.

HISTORICAL ROMANCE

Teens enjoy many of the same historical romances as adults. While for several years little effort was made to publish historical romance for teens, the trend is changing. Keep in mind that historical to a teen is anything before she or he was born.

Armstrong, Jennifer. Wild Rose Inn series: *Ann of the Wild Rose Inn, 1774, Bridie of the Wild Rose Inn, 1695, Emily of the Wild Rose Inn, 1858.* and *Laura of the Wild Rose Inn, 1898.* Several generations of MacKenzie girls grow up in Marblehead Inn.

Esquivel, Laura. *Like Water for Chocolate*. A young woman in frontier Mexico is denied the man she loves when her mother forces him to marry her sister. *Like Water for Chocolate* made ALA's Best Books for Young Adults list after being nominated by a teen. She loved the book so much that she solicited comments on it from all her friends who had read it to pass on to the committee.

Garland, Sherry. *Song of the Buffalo Boy*. Loi's life, difficult because of her American blood, is further complicated when she is forbidden to marry Khai, the boy she has always loved. She runs away to Ho Chi Minh City to avoid marriage to the odious Heip.

Hobbs, Valerie. *How Far Would You Have Gotten If I Hadn't Called You Back?* Bron finds love and drag racing in California of the 1950s.

Kincaid, Nancy. *Crossing Blood*. Lucy falls in love with the maid's son in a time and place that forbids interracial love. *Crossing Blood* is another adult title that made the Best Books list. It was also selected as an outstanding romance by the YALSA Romance Genre committee.

Magorian, Michelle. *Not a Swan*. Three sisters learn about life as they live in an English seaside town during World War II.

Qualey, Marsha. *Come in from the Cold*. The Vietnam war has taken something very precious away from both Maud and Jeff. She lost her sister through the protest movement and he lost his brother in the fighting.

Smith, Nancy Covert. Apple Valley series. DeLanna Robinsohn comes of age on a farm in western Pennsylvania in the early nineteenth century.

Watson, Jude. The Brides of Wildcat County series: *Dangerous: Savannah's Story, Scandalous: Eden's Story,* and *Impetuous: Mattie's Story.* The tales of three young women who go to the gold fields of California as mail-order brides.

ADULT ROMANCE FOR TEENS

Teens read many adult romances, in addition to books written specifically for teens. The following are just a few that have found popularity with teens.

Romantic Suspense

The combination of love and danger is a heady one. The adventure and mysteries encountered by the heroines do not diminish the romance. The following authors have written several books in this genre for adults that are read by teens:

Clark, Mary Higgins

Hodge, Jane Aiken

Holt, Victoria

Howatch, Susan

Johnston, Velda

Lofts, Norah

Michaels, Barbara

Seton, Anya

Stewart, Mary

Whitney, Phyllis

Regency Romance

The mannered romance of the "ton" features elaborate balls and the apparel to go with them. Beautiful young women in empire dresses come out for a season to find a rakish young man who will settle down to marriage.

Cartland, Barbara

Chesney, Marion

Heyer, Georgette

Veryan, Patricia

Time Travel Fantasy Romance

The books that fall into this category use time travel as a backdrop for the romance. The obstacle facing the lovers is not merely one of having different backgrounds or living in different time zones, but the difficulty of living in different centuries. This is a very popular type in paperback, but is also published in hardcover. The ones that seem to have the most teen appeal are the thickest ones!

Deveraux, Jude. *Knight in Shining Armor*. Tears at a crypt bring a medieval knight into the present.

Gabaldon, Diana. *Outlander. Dragonfly in Amber. Voyager.*

Christian Historical Romance

The Christian romances have been heavily marketed in supermarkets, with the result that they became very popular with readers before many librarians caught on to the trend. Published by Christian presses like Bethany House and Harvest House, they have only recently become available through jobbers and are still not widely reviewed. Ingrams has a catalog called *Christian Advance*.

The stories usually feature young women who face a series of trials and troubles in their marriages and, through their faith, realize a positive ending. Popular authors of Christian historical romances are:

Bacher, June Masters. Heartland Heritage series. Pioneer series.

Feldhake, Susan C. Enduring Faith series.

Morris, Gilbert. Liberty Bell series. House of Winslow series.

Oke, Janette. Canadian West Saga. Women of the West series. Love Comes Softly series. Seasons of the Heart series.

Peart, Jane. Brides of Montclair series. Westward Dreams series. Orphan Train series.

Pella, Judith, and Michael R. Phillips. Russians series. Journals of Corrie Belle Hollister series. Stonewycke Legacy series. Highlander Collection series.

Thoene, Bodie. Shiloh Legacy series. Zion Covenant series. Zion Chronicles series.

TOPICS

YALSA Romance Genre List

Block, Francesca Lia. *Weetzie Bat.* HarperTrophy. $3.95 (ISBN 0-06-447068-7). For punk teen Weetzie Bat and her unusual L.A. friends, life is a magical search for love and friendship.

Bonner, Cindy. *Lily: A Love Story.* NAL/Dutton. $4.99 (ISBN 0-451-404394). Are the townspeople right when they call Lily's exciting new love a murderer?

Bridgers, Sue Ellen. *Permanent Connections.* HarperTrophy. $3.95 (ISBN 0-06-447020-2). Rebellious and moody, Rob is sent to live with relatives in rural North Carolina where he meets the difficult and equally unhappy Ellery.

Brooks, Martha. *Two Moons in August.* Scholastic Point. $3.25 (ISBN 0-590-45923-6). Sidonie slowly begins to recover from the death of her mother when she meets and falls in love with Kieran, the new boy in town.

Caseley, Judith. *Kisses.* Random. $3.99 (ISBN 0-679-82672-6). Following a string of unhappy dates, unwanted advances, and secret love notes, Hannah's search for the perfect boyfriend comes to an end.

Clements, Bruce. *Tom Loves Anna Loves Tom.* Farrar, Straus & Giroux. $3.95 (ISBN 0-374-47939-9). Though they share only two weeks together, Anna and Tom know their love will last a lifetime.

Cooney, Caroline B. *Forbidden*. Scholastic. $3.50 (ISBN 0-590-46574-0). Meet Annabel and Daniel—a beautiful, wealthy couple whose love is shadowed by a murderous past and dark family secrets.

du Maurier, Daphne. *Rebecca*. Avon. $5.99 (ISBN 0-380-00917-X). After marrying handsome Maxim, the new Mrs. DeWinter finds herself living in the chilling shadow of his first wife, Rebecca, who died under mysterious circumstances.

Garden, Nancy. *Annie on My Mind*. Farrar, Straus & Giroux. $3.95 (ISBN 0-374-40414-3). Annie and Liza love the Metropolitan Museum of Art, medieval history, acting, and . . . each other.

Hahn, Mary D. *The Wind Blows Backwards*. Avon Flare. $3.99 (ISBN 0-380-77530-1). Can rekindling an old love save Spencer's life?

Irwin, Hadley. *Abby, My Love*. Signet Vista. $2.50 (ISBN 0-451-14501-1). When Chip falls in love with Abby, he is puzzled by her cold behavior until he discovers her tragic secret.

Kincaid, Nancy. *Crossing Blood*. Avon. $10.00 (ISBN 0-380-72111-2). In the 1960s South, where interracial love is forbidden, Lucy and Skippy spend their days watching and wanting from a distance.

Kindl, Patrice. *Owl in Love*. Puffin. $3.99 (ISBN 0-14-037129-X). Owl's ability to change from girl to bird creates complications when she falls in love with a strange boy she discovers in the woods.

Klause, Annette Curtis. *The Silver Kiss*. Dell. $3.99 (ISBN 0-440-21346-0). When Zoe most needs a friend, she meets Simon, a sexy, 300-year-old vampire on a mission of revenge!

Mazer, Harry. *The Girl of His Dreams*. Avon Flare. $2.95 (ISBN 0-380-70599-0). Willis's fantasy of the perfect, loving girlfriend is challenged when he meets plain, outspoken Sophie, hardly the "girl of his dreams"—or is she?

McKinley, Robin. *Beauty*. HarperTrophy. $4.95 (ISBN 0-06-440477-3). Held captive in an enchanted castle, Beauty has every comfort, plus the love of the hideously ugly but charming Beast.

Pascal, Francine. *Love & Betrayal & Hold the Mayo*. Dell. $2.95 (ISBN 0-440-94735-9). An already disastrous summer camp experience takes a turn for the worse when Victoria realizes she's in love with her best friend's boyfriend.

Powell, Randy. *Is Kissing a Girl Who Smokes Like Licking an Ashtray?* Farrar, Straus & Giroux. $3.95 (ISBN 0-374-43627-4). Biff thinks he's in love with Tommie until he meets the beautiful, wild, and cigarette-smoking Heidi.

Sonnenmark, Laura. *Something's Rotten in the State of Maryland*. Scholastic. $2.95 (ISBN 0-590-42877-2). When Marie's play is chosen for production, she is determined that Simon, the pretentious director, will steal neither her lines nor her heart.

Westall, Robert. *The Promise.* Scholastic. $3.25 (ISBN 0-590-43761-5). A romance reaches beyond the grave when Valerie's ghost returns to remind Bob of his promise to join her in death.

Alternates in Priority Order

Martin, Ann. *Just a Summer Romance.* Scholastic. $2.75 (ISBN 0-590-43999-5). Melanie is shocked when she discovers that the boy she loved last summer and is trying to forget is now a hot new television star!

Carter, Alden R. *Up Country.* Scholastic Point. $2.95 (ISBN 0-590-43638-4). Despite their differences, city-smart Carl and country-smart Signa find themselves falling in love.

Willey, Margaret. *Saving Lenny.* Bantam. $2.99 (ISBN 0-553-29204-8). If only she could love Lenny enough, Jesse thinks, his depression would lift and they could live happily ever after.

Hudson, Jan. *Sweetgrass.* Scholastic. $2.95 (ISBN 0-590-43486-1). Sweetgrass yearns to marry Eagle Sun, but she must first prove her strength before she's allowed to follow her heart.

Garland, Sherry. *Song of the Buffalo Boy.* Harcourt Brace. $3.95 (ISBN 0-15-200098-4). Vietnamese American Loi is in love with Khai but both are promised to others. How can they teach their families to understand the meaning of love?

Daly, Maureen. *Seventeenth Summer.* Archway. $3.50 (ISBN 0-671-61931-4). As one special summer draws to an end, Angie is tempted to trade her dream of college for the love of a small-town boy.

Smith, Betty. *Joy in the Morning.* HarperCollins. $6.00 (ISBN 0-06-080368-1). They're young and penniless, but despite their parents' objections Annie and Carl are determined to marry and share their lives forever.

Kingsolver, Barbara. *Animal Dreams.* Harper Perennial. $10.00 (ISBN 0-06-092114-5). Codi returns to a hometown filled with memories of Lloyd and a passion that cannot be forgotten.

Gabaldon, Diana. *Outlander.* Dell. $5.99 (ISBN 0-440-21256-1). Claire is happily married until the fateful day she is hurled back in time to be courted by a passionate Scots warrior.

Cohen, Barbara. *People Like Us.* Bantam. $2.95 (ISBN 0-553-27445-7). Dinah's parents are upset because she is dating outside her religion, but it is finally up to her to decide between pleasing her family and following her heart.

YALSA Romance Genre Committee: Judy Sasges, Monroe, WA, Chair; Margaret L. Butzler, Bethel Park, PA; Diane P. Monnier, Germantown, MD; Nina O'Donnell, Honolulu, HI; Jan Sarratt, Gaffney, SC; Evelyn C. Walker, Mt. Vernon, IN.

D's Picks

Bauer, Joan. *Squashed.*

Davis, Jenny. *Sex Education.*

Garland, Sherry. *Song of the Buffalo Boy.*

Hahn, Mary Downing. *The Wind Blows Backwards.*

Qualey, Marsha. *Revolutions of the Heart.*

Index